ARCHAEOLOGICAL TEST EXCAVATIONS
IN SOUTHERN ARIZONA

Compiled by

Susan A. Brew

Contributions by

Allen Dart
Suzanne K. Fish
James Gibb
Bruce B. Huckell
Lisa W. Huckell
Charles H. Miksicek
Earl W. Sires

Submitted by

Cultural Resource Management Division
Arizona State Museum
The University of Arizona

December 1981

Archaeological Series No. 152

PREFACE

In the course of a year, the Cultural Resource Management Division (CRMD) of the Arizona State Museum (ASM) completes many "service" projects in southern Arizona. These projects, which take as little as an hour or as long as a week to complete, usually involve inventory survey work and are often associated with construction of housing and related utilities (water, electric, sewer). These surveys, although more variable in their contribution to archaeological information than those of larger scope, are nevertheless important. We strongly believe that archaeologists and proponents of legislation for historic preservation must help developers comply with state and federal preservation laws, and must do so in a timely, thorough, and cost-effective manner.

Because of the large number of service projects and the special problems they pose--for example, large amounts of paperwork relative to project size, and inexperience with historic preservation laws on the part of many sponsors--the CRMD employs Project Directors who are specialists in this field. The scope of work that defines such projects has been formalized within the CRMD and is available to interested persons.

When an inventory survey locates archaeological sites that cannot be adequately assessed by surface examination alone, subsurface testing is recommended to determine site depth, extent, function, significance, and eligibility for inclusion on the State or National Register of Historic Places. Of nearly 100 inventory surveys I have directed since 1978, 20 have gone on to later testing phases. A list of the survey and testing projects conducted in the past two years has been prepared for the Arizona Archaeological Council and is published within their bibliographies of Arizona archaeology for 1979 and 1980.

Service projects usually generate short letter reports which languish in project files. This volume is a sample of testing project reports and was compiled to bring project data from the files to the attention of professionals and interested laymen.

Service projects have given the CRMD many opportunities to study a wide range of prehistoric and historic cultural manifestations. Data gathered during projects like the ones in this volume not only have enhanced our cumulative knowledge of the history and prehistory of southern Arizona, but have stimulated interesting and creative archaeological research.

The first report in this volume, "Archaeological testing at
AZ AA:112:117, the Rancho del Cerro quarry site," by Earl W. Sires,
details the first test excavations at an Archaic lithic quarry site in
the Tucson Basin. The project provided valuable data for comparison
with data from testing operations at similar sites, including those in
the northeastern Santa Rita Mountains that were tested for the ANAMAX-
Rosemont project. Comparative data are rare because investigation of
lithic procurement sites in southern Arizona has been minimal. Projects
of this kind can only expand our knowledge of prehistoric exploitation
of natural resources within the Tucson Basin, an area with limited
sources of workable lithic material.

"Archaeological testing at AZ AA:16:44, the Salida del Sol
Hohokam site," by Allen Dart, was undertaken to determine site integrity,
site depth, and intra-site organization, and to prepare for the data
recovery phase that would be inevitable if the developers exercised
their option to purchase and develop the site area. Surface inspection
revealed a large, complex site from the Classic Period (Tanque Verde
Phase) of the Tucson Basin Hohokam sequence. Testing methods for this
project were similar to those used during recent excavations undertaken
by the CRMD along the Salt-Gila Aqueduct (Teague and Crown 1980). This
methodology proved to be extremely efficient.

"Archaeological collection and testing at AZ EE:7:22, a site in
the Babocomari Valley, Cochise County, Arizona," by Allen Dart, details
test excavations at a site consisting of an artifact scatter and associated roasting pit. I have included it in this volume as an example
of the interesting, creative research that can be done with limited data
from a small site. The use of a model advanced by Goodyear (1975) for
the pottery analysis, and a model advanced by Bayham (1976) for the
lithic analysis, led to the conclusion that this site was a temporary
camp and a wild food processing site. Subsequent pollen and flotation
analysis results supported and refined this conclusion and illustrated
the usefulness of such models in guiding the analysis of artifact
assemblages from limited activity sites.

"Archaeological test excavations at Tubac State Park, Arizona,"
by Bruce and Lisa Huckell, was included in this volume for yet another
reason. Through the years, many people have been interested in the
Spanish and Mexican periods in Arizona. The Arizona State Museum has
undertaken a good deal of archaeological work in the village of Tubac,
which was an important center during those periods (Shenk and Teague
1975). This report supplements the reports generated by those earlier
studies.

Finally, "An archaeological investigation of AZ BB:13:146, a
small occupation site in the Tucson Basin, Pima County, Arizona," by
Allen Dart and others, describes the excavation of a small Rincon Phase
farmstead. The single pit house at the site contained an unusually well-
preserved floor assemblage of artifacts, features, and botanical remains.
This assemblage provided a unique opportunity to study the internal

spatial organization of the house, because the artifact and feature arrangements suggested activities that were occurring immediately prior to the house's destruction. Food remains in the house, including three varieties of corn and domesticated beans, seeds of wild plant foods, and bones of wild game, provided a rare insight into Rincon Phase Hohokam diet in the Tucson Basin.

This volume serves as a reminder that small archaeological projects, generated by preservation legislation such as the National Environmental Policy Act of 1969, can be completed promptly and efficiently, and that they can provide the basis for creative, productive archaeological research that may contribute significantly to our knowledge of the history and prehistory of southern Arizona.

Yet the research potential of such small excavation projects does not end here. It became apparent during the compilation of this volume that data gathered during testing phases is now plentiful and forms a substantial body of information pertinent to a wide variety of research concerns. For example, an examination of the relationships between site locations, surface characteristics, and the presence or absence of subsurface features, could contribute to the development of models for predicting site types and locations. Such models would be useful in both management and research contexts. Each of the studies in this volume stands as an individual contribution, but may also be viewed as a potential building block for future research projects of much broader scale.

Susan A. Brew
Project Director

ACKNOWLEDGMENTS

Many people have contributed to the completion of this volume and the five testing projects described herein. First and foremost, we wish to acknowledge our Sponsors: Solmar Investment Corporation, Pulte Home Corporation, Arizona State Parks, and Huachuca City, for their interest in preserving Arizona's cultural heritage. We appreciate having the opportunity to undertake these studies.

Several editors have worked to create a cohesive volume from a potpourri of project reports. Marcia Davis, Benjamin Smith, and Joseph Stevens deserve many pats on the back for their efforts. Thanks are also extended to Brian Byrd who did the project illustrations and María Abdín and Nephi Bushman who typed multiple versions of these manuscripts with nary a whimper.

I also wish to thank my friends and co-workers Jon Czaplicki, Bruce B. Huckell, David A. Gregory, and Lynn S. Teague. They were always available to share ideas and expertise and to provide moral support. The prevailing atmosphere of sharing and caring makes working for CRMD extremely rewarding and, to quote an anonymous intellectual giant, "a real good time."

Finally, following a long-standing academic tradition pointed out to me by my spouse during negotiations about who would pick up the tab for the celebration honoring this volume's completion, I must acknowledge my husband. This acknowledgment is a small price to pay for his unfailing good humor, maintained even when crew members called during dinner to discuss project problems of major import, such as what to do tomorrow if the backhoe operator still has the flu. For all counseling services rendered, occasional volunteer archaeological services, legal advice, moral support, and the celebration dinner, thank you Lindsay Brew.

Susan A. Brew
Project Director

CONTENTS

CHAPTERS

CHAPTER 1

ARCHAEOLOGICAL TESTING AT AZ AA:112:117,
THE RANCHO DEL CERRO QUARRY SITE

by

Earl W. Sires

for

Solmar Investment Corporation

The Cultural Resource Management Division
Arizona State Museum
University of Arizona

June 1980

Table of Contents

List of Figures

List of Tables

Introduction

On June 12 and 13, 1980, Arizona State Museum archaeologists Lisa W. Huckell and Earl W. Sires conducted an archaeological testing program at AZ AA:12:117, a lithic quarry site. This program was designed to determine the nature and distribution of surface artifacts as well as the depth of cultural material. In addition, the site's research potential, significance, and eligibility for inclusion on the National Register of Historic Places were assessed.

Lisa W. Huckell performed an archaeological clearance survey for Solmar Investment Corporation on June 2 and 3, 1980. The area surveyed included some 300 acres slated for residential development. During the course of the survey, AZ AA:12:117 was recorded, and additional work at this site in the form of a testing program was recommended. Mr. Terry Klipp, President of Solmar Investment Corporation, authorized the Arizona State Museum to conduct this program, which included the recording of surface artifacts and features, limited subsurface excavation, and analysis of an artifact collection from the site.

Physical Setting

The site is located on the northwest side of the city of Tucson, Arizona, in the NE 1/4 of the NE 1/4 of Section 23, T13S, R12E, at the intersection of El Camino del Cerro and Gerhart Road (Figure 1). It measures approximately 45 m by 100 m and lies within the boundaries of House Lot Number 380 of the planned Rancho del Cerro subdivision (Figure 2). It is unknown what effect the construction of Camino del Cerro and Gerhart Roads may have had upon additional cultural resources associated with the site.

AZ AA:12:117 is situated within the dissected eastern pediment of the Tucson Mountains on a broad northeast-trending ridge at the contact between Pleistocene alluvial deposits and a porphyritic igneous bedrock outcrop. The soil consists of a fine sandy matrix containing boulder gravels and unconsolidated bedrock exposures. The site surface slopes gently to the northwest toward a small ephemeral wash that lies at the base of an unconsolidated bedrock knoll (Figure 3).

The site is located within the lower Sonoran Lifezone in the Paloverde/Saguaro plant community (Lowe 1964). In addition to these species, creosote-bush, triangle bursage, and barrel, prickly pear, and cholla cacti are present. A dense desert riparian plant community containing such additional species as mesquite, catclaw acacia, smoketree, and desert hackberry is found in the large washes of the area.

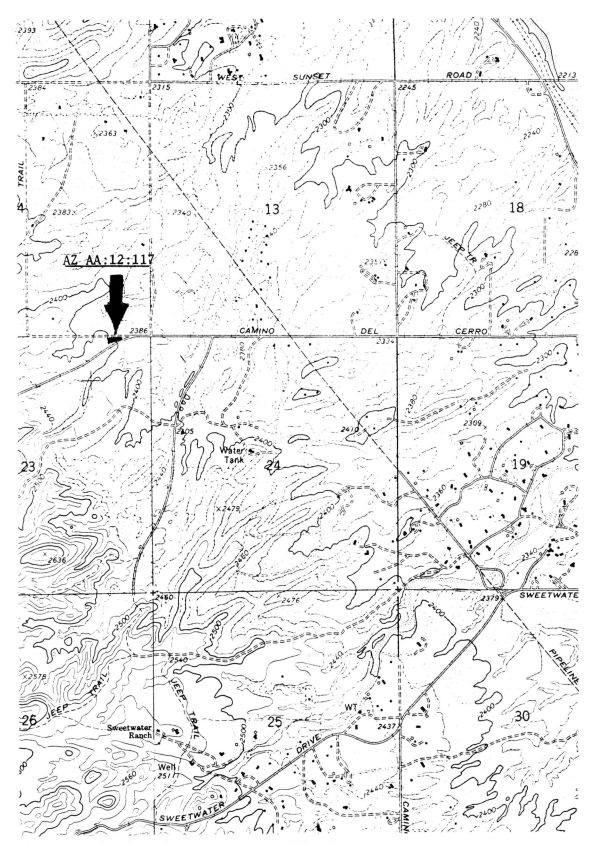

Figure 1. The location of AZ AA:12:117, the Rancho del Cerro quarry site

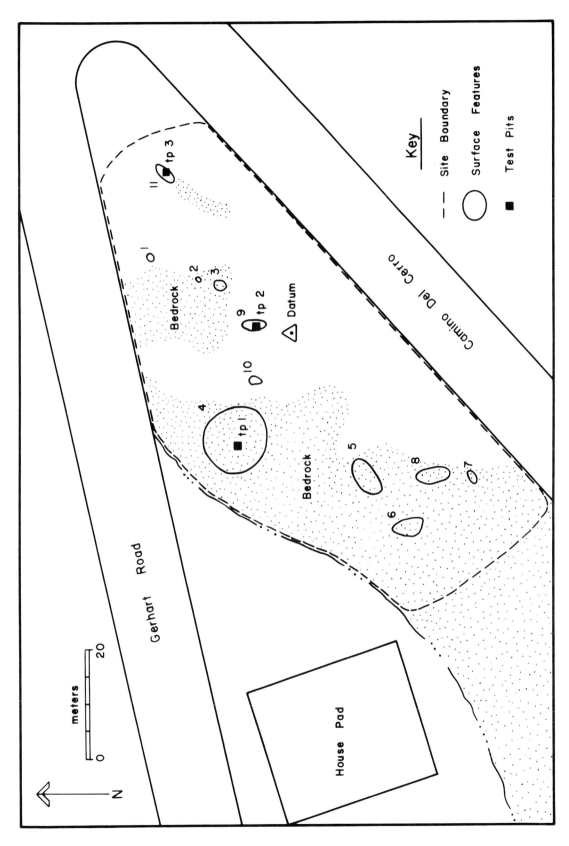

Figure 2. AZ AA:12:117, the Rancho del Cerro quarry site

Figure 3.   General view of AZ AA:12:117, looking east

Figure 4.   Feature 6, looking northeast

Methodology

Site boundaries were determined by the archaeologists walking a
series of parallel transects spaced at 10-m intervals. The point at
which artifact density decreased significantly was noted and considered
the boundary. While it was found that lithic and, to a much lesser
degree, ceramic artifacts were thinly distributed throughout the site,
11 spatially distinct artifact concentrations were identified. Eight
of these (Features 1 through 8, Figure 2) were composed solely of lithic
materials; the remaining three (Features 9 through 11, Figure 2) were
small sherd clusters. Artifact samples were collected from Features 4
through 9, and 11. The smaller features were collected completely, while
representative samples were collected from the larger, more dense features. Selected isolated artifacts were collected as well.

To determine the depth of cultural material at the site, three
1 m-by-1 m test units were excavated. These were placed within areas of
high artifact density that were considered to hold the greatest potential
for cultural depth (Figure 2). Test Unit 1 was placed within Feature 4;
Test Units 2 and 3 were excavated within Features 9 and 10 respectively.
Finally, a map indicating site location, the extent and distribution of
surface features, and the location of test pits was prepared using a
plane table and alidade.

Surface Features

Lithic Artifact Concentrations

With the exception of Feature 1, all lithic artifact concentrations were located within the boundaries of unconsolidated bedrock
outcrops which were visible as concentrated areas of boulder gravels
(Figure 4). These features ranged in size from less than 1 m to over
12 m in diameter. The materials selected for reduction were primarily
rhyolites. Quartzite, basalt, silicified limestone, andesite, and chert
were also used. Artifact type frequencies were fairly consistent
between all features, consisting primarily of debitage and core fragments.
Cores and retouched flakes accounted for 6 percent of the total assemblage.

The range of raw materials and variation in the degree of patination observed on the artifacts suggest that the majority of the lithic
artifact concentrations are the result of re-use of a particular reduction
locus over a considerable period of time. The single exception to this
is Feature 8, in which more than 96 percent of the raw material was a
rhyolite with a distinctive, well-developed, yellow brown patina indicating a single reduction event.

Ceramic Concentrations

Features 9, 10, and 11 were small sherd clusters containing an average of 10 plain ware sherds each. The location of these features was recorded and all sherds from Features 9 and 11 were collected. Feature 10 sherds were not collected. Feature 9 contained 12 sherds with brown exteriors, a fine, sandy, somewhat micaceous paste, and a prominent carbon streak in the core. Ten sherds were recovered from Feature 11. These exhibited an orange-fired exterior and a smuged interior surface with a coarse, sandy paste. Both ceramic types were locally produced and in each feature related to a single vessel. Since these were small body sherds, vessel shape could not be determined.

In addition to the ceramic assemblage discussed above, a single red-on-brown sherd was recovered just east of Feature 8. The small size of this sherd prohibited its assignment to a particular ceramic type. However, it can be stated that it is a locally produced type dating to sometime between A.D. 700 and 1300--the Rillito through Tanque Verde Phases of the Tucson Basin Hohokam chronological sequence.

Test Excavations

As mentioned previously, three 1 m-by-1 m test pits were placed in areas of high artifact density in order to investigate possible sub-surface cultural deposits. Test Pit 1 was excavated within Feature 4 at the point where a rhyolite biface with associated flakes had been recorded (Figure 7). The pit was excavated to a depth of 10 cm; fill consisted of unconsolidated bedrock blocks and small amounts of sandy soil. Three flakes, identical in material type and patination to those associated with the biface, were recovered. Test Pits 2 and 3 were placed within Features 9 and 11, respectively. Test Pit 2 was excavated to a depth of 10 cm, while Test Pit 3 was excavated to a depth of only 5 cm. Neither pit yielded artifacts. The results of these excavations indicate that the presence of subsurface deposits at AZ AA:12:117 is unlikely. The fact that three flakes were recovered in Test Pit 1 is best explained by the effects of erosion or animal disturbance causing their burial subsequent to deposition.

Artifact Assemblage

Table 1 summarizes the 301 pieces of flaked stone recovered from the site. Although six raw material types were identified within the assemblage, the predominant raw material was a gray, medium-grained rhyolite that occurs in unconsolidated outcrops on the site. The faulted and fractured nature of the raw material is reflected by the fact that over 50 percent of the assemblage consists of core and flake fragments and shatter.

Table 1. Flaked stone analysis: AZ AA:12:117

Raw Material	Debitage					Retouched Flakes			Cores				Total	Frequency
	Primary	Secondary	Tertiary	Flake Fragments/ Shatter	Total	Unifacial	Bifacial	Total	Single Platform	Globular	Fragments	Total		
Rhyolite	15	20	71	120	226	3	4	7	2	4	16	22	255	85%
Quartzite	1	3	3	5	12	2	-	2		1	-	1	15	5%
Basalt	1	1	2	7	11	-	-	-	-	-	1	1	12	4%
Silicified Limestone	-	5	1	3	9	-	2	2	1	-	-	1	12	4%
Andesite	1	2	1	-	4	-	-	-	-	-	1	1	5	2%
Chert	-	1	-	1	2	-	-	-	-	-	-	-	2	<1%
Total	18	32	78	136	264	5	6	11	3	5	18	26	301	
Frequency	6%	11%	26%	45%	88%	1%	2%	3%	1%	2%	6%	9%		

The vast majority of the assemblage is composed of reduction debitage with retouched specimens accounting for only 3 percent of the total. Of the five unifaces recovered (Figure 8), none fit formal tool categories. They are simply flakes with limited marginal retouch. While it is possible these functioned as implements, they may also represent efforts at testing the potential of a particular flake for further modification.

Bifacially retouched artifacts included two flakes with only limited retouch, and four morphologically similar specimens that had been more extensively flaked (Figures 5 and 6). The latter were produced by hard-hammer percussion, evidenced by the relatively deep flake scars and crushed platforms. The cause of discard, either step fractures or natural imperfections in the raw material, is apparent in all cases. Table 2 presents the dimensions and raw material type for the bifaces.

Table 2. Biface measurements: AZ AA:12:117

Biface	Length	Width	Thickness	Raw Material
a	9.2 cm	6.1 cm	2.3 cm	Silicifed limestone
b	8.6 cm	5.5 cm	2.9 cm	Silicified limestone
c	9.5 cm	5.8 cm	3.3 cm	Rhyolite
d	9.7 cm	5.8 cm	3.2 cm	Rhyolite

All but one of the eight cores recovered were located within surface features. They included five globular and three single platform specimens (Figure 10a, c). Size ranged from 20 cm by 18 cm by 11 cm to less than 7 cm in maximum dimension. All except one had the potential for further flake removal.

Of the total of 128 whole flakes recovered, 63 percent were tertiary flakes. However, a relatively high percentage of primary and secondary flakes were present as well. To quickly obtain information on relative flake size, whole flakes were placed within a series of consecutively larger squares drawn on graph paper. While there was considerable variation in flake size both within and between flake types, this method resulted in average sizes of 27 square centimeters for primary flakes, 17 square centimeters for secondary flakes, and 11 square centimeters for tertiary flakes. Flake morphology indicates that hard-hammer percussion was the principal means of reduction employed at the site.

Patination varied greatly on both retouched specimens and debitage. Rhyolite ranged in surface appearance from a "fresh" gray to a dull,

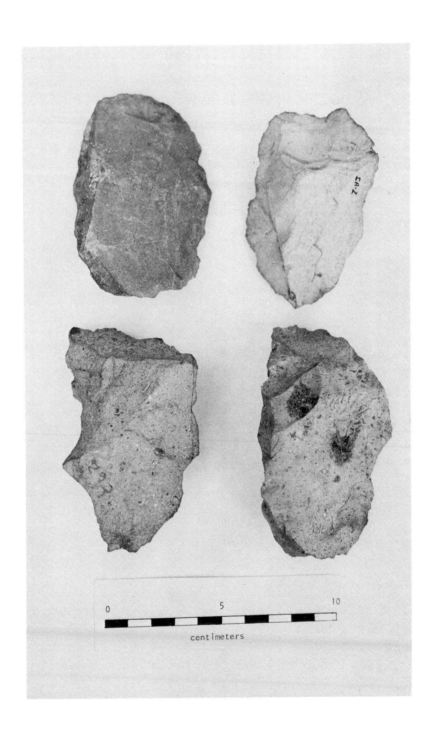

Figure 5. Bifaces from AZ AA:12:117; a, b) silicified limestone; c, d) rhyolite

Figure 6. View of reverse side of bifaces

Figure 8. Unifacially retouched flakes from AZ AA:12:117; a, b) quartzite; c, d, e) rhyolite

Figure 7. Biface and sample of associated flakes from Feature 4

Figure 10. Lithic artifacts from AZ AA:12:117; a) quartzite hammer-stone; b) globular core (rhyolite); c) single platform core from Feature 5 (rhyolite)

Figure 9. Large quartzite core from Feature 5

yellow brown well-developed patina. Silicified limestone ranged from blue-gray to a chalky brown weathered surface. All bifaces exhibited substantial patination, reaching an extreme on the specimen recovered from Feature 5 (Figures 5a and 6a) on which the flake scars are obscure.

Conclusions

On the basis of the ratio of debitage to retouched flakes, the absence of implements and the relatively high frequency of primary and secondary flakes, AZ AA:12:117 can be identified as a quarry site. Eight reduction loci were identified. Seven of these experienced repeated use, while the eighth was the result of a single reduction event. Since good sources of workable material are rare within the Tucson Basin, it is likely that this quarry was exploited at intervals over a long period of time, as is evidenced by the variation in artifact patination. That occupation of the site was of limited duration and intensity is evidenced by the lack of cultural depth. While no diagnostic artifacts were present, indications of Archaic Period use are found in the presence of heavily patinated bifaces. In addition, similar raw material types are abundant at the Silverbell Site, a Cochise Culture base camp located south of AZ AA:12:117 along the Santa Cruz River (Bruce Huckell, Arizona State Museum, personal communication). The absence of biface thinning flakes and the relatively crude nature of the bifaces suggests that raw material was reduced to form bifacial preforms, which were transported elsewhere, probably to base camps, for further modification and tool production.

Use of the quarry during the Ceramic Period is evidenced by the presence of a small quantity of sherds and a quartzite flaked hammerstone, a type frequently found at ceramic sites (see Haury 1976:279-280) (Figure 10a). Lithic artifacts lacking patination also attest to this more recent use.

Recommendations

In southern Arizona, investigation of lithic procurement sites such as AZ AA:12:117 has been minimal. Although testing operations at a number of quarry sites in the northeastern Santa Rita Mountains have recently taken place (Huckell 1980), quarry sites within the Tucson Basin have remained uninvestigated. Consequently, AZ AA:12:117 can provide significant comparative data concerning prehistoric exploitation of lithic resources in southern Arizona. In addition, this information can expand existing knowledge concerning the exploitation of natural resources within the Tucson Basin. An artifact sample sufficient to allow further investigation has, however, been collected and the site has been adequately mapped. It is felt, therefore, that AZ AA:12:117 does not warrant inclusion on the National Register of Historic Places, and that it holds little potential to yield additional information of archaeological significance.

The Arizona State Museum recommends clearance for construction of House Lot No. 380, on which AZ AA:12:117 is located, and recommends clearance for the construction of the Rancho del Cerro subdivision.

CHAPTER 2

ARCHAEOLOGICAL TESTING AT AZ AA:16:44,
THE SALIDA DEL SOL HOHOKAM SITE

by

Allen Dart

for

Pulte Home Corporation

The Cultural Resource Management Division
Arizona State Museum
University of Arizona

August 1980

Table of Contents

List of Figures

List of Tables

Introduction

From August 11 through August 13, 1980, Arizona State Museum archaeologists Elizabeth Henderson and Allen Dart conducted an archaeological testing program at AZ AA:16:44, a Hohokam Indian habitation site. The program was carried out to determine the nature and distribution of surface artifacts, the depth of cultural materials, and the nature and depth of any architectural features. The site's research potential, significance, and eligibility for inclusion on the National Register of Historic Places were also assessed.

An archaeological clearance survey for Pulte Home Corporation had been conducted by Edward M. Fortier and Lyle M. Stone in April, 1980. The survey area included approximately 60 acres of land, which is the proposed site of Salida del Sol, a 270-unit housing subdivision. AZ AA:16:44 was recorded during that inspection, and additional work to further evaluate this cultural resource was recommended. Mr. Frank Della, Area Manager for Pulte Home Corporation, authorized the Arizona State Museum to conduct this additional work, which included recording surface artifacts and features, limited subsurface excavations, and analysis of an artifact collection from the site.

Physical Setting

AZ AA:16:44 is located southwest of the City of Tucson, Arizona, in the NW 1/4 of the SE 1/4 of Section 16, T15S, R13E, on and around the intersection of Westover Avenue and Corona Road, and eastward onto the San Xavier Papago Indian Reservation (Figure 1). The portion of the site studied in the testing program is located between Corona Road on the south and an El Paso Natural Gas Company pipeline on the north, and from the San Xavier Reservation boundary fence on the east to an imaginary line about 250 m west of the fence, a total area of approximately 26,000 square meters (6.4 acres). The site is situated on a broad, alluviated plain which slopes gently eastward toward the Santa Cruz River, in a vegetation association of creosote and desert grasses with occasional barrel and cholla cacti (Figure 2). Tumbleweeds and small, ground-covering plants are growing on areas disturbed by grading. Nearly half of the site portion under study has been disturbed by road and pipeline easement blading and excavation.

Methodology

Field archaeologists inspected the site area to determine the boundaries of the artifact concentration. The boundaries were pinflagged;

24

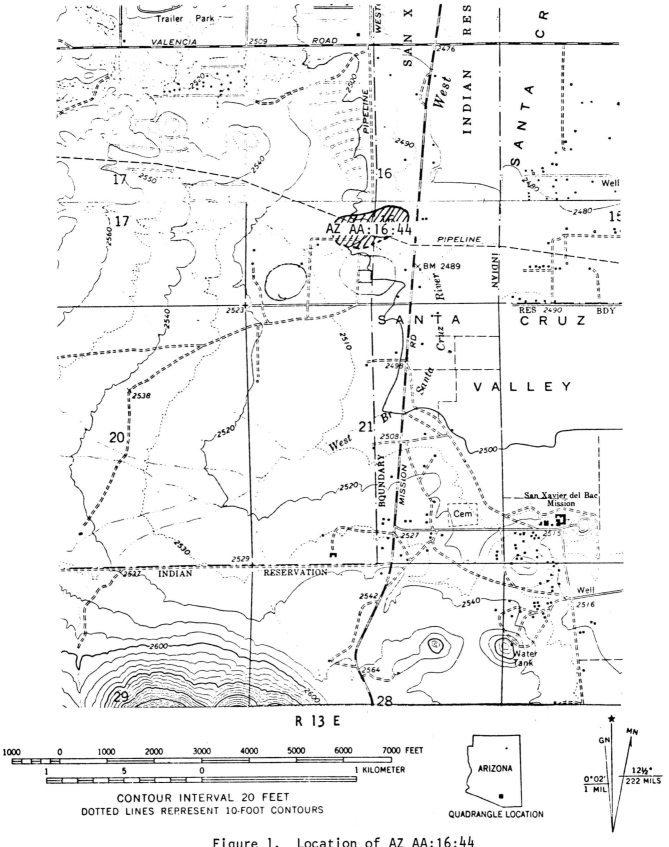

Figure 1. Location of AZ AA:16:44

Figure 2. Environmental setting of
AZ AA:16:44

then an arbitrary grid system was laid out using an alidade. A reference
datum was established, and all artifact concentrations as well as modern
structures in the study area were mapped with reference to the arbitrary
datum. Two base lines were established, one running magnetic north at
150 m east of the datum, and one running 90 degrees eastward at 100 m
north of the datum. Wooden stakes were set at 10-m intervals along these
two lines (Figure 3). The arbitrary datum itself was not staked.

After the grid lines were established, a site map was made using
alidade and plane table. The 1-m wide sample transects were set running
northward at 10-m intervals. In each transect, the density of artifacts
was recorded for every 1-m square, and artifacts in every tenth square
were totally collected. The density of artifacts over the entire study
area was sampled in this manner, and areas of greater artifact density
were determined. One percent of the surface artifacts were collected,
and 10 percent were recorded as to number per square meter.

After areas of greater and lesser artifact densities were plotted
on a graph, this information was used to select areas for subsurface
testing. One backhoe trench (Trench 1) was excavated in an area of low
artifact density, and two others (Trenches 2 and 3) were placed in higher
density areas. After excavation, the faces of the trenches were examined
for the presence of architectural features and to determine the depth of
cultural deposits. Where architectural features were observed in the
trench faces, profile drawings were made. Artifacts excavated by the
backhoe were collected, and all trenches were backfilled after study was
completed. A grab sample of diagnostic artifacts from the site was collected at random; in addition, some local amateur archaeologists, John
and Randy Owens, donated materials they had collected from the site.

Test Excavations

Test Trench 1 was placed 120 m east of the site datum, between 65.2 m and 69.5 m north of datum (Figure 3), and it was excavated to a depth of 70 cm below surface. The top 30 cm of deposit in this trench was a brown silty sand mixed with gravel. From 30 cm to 70 cm below surface there was a hard caliche layer. No features were observed in Trench 1, and only five sherds were recovered from the excavated dirt.

Trench 2 was placed approximately 146 m east and from 65 m to 74 m north of datum, running true north for 9.8 m (Figure 3). This trench was placed at the east edge of an area previously excavated by local collectors, who suggested to the field archaeologists that a pit house was there. A house floor with adobe wall remnants was observed in the west face of Trench 2, and a profile drawing was made (Figure 4). Only 11 sherds were observed in the excavated dirt, and these were collected.

Trench 3 was placed between 68.5 m and 86.2 m north, and 179 m and 180 m east of datum. This area was selected due to a higher artifact density than most other areas of the site. Another house floor was indicated in this trench by the presence of a layer of ashy dirt 3 m long and up to 25 cm thick, observable in both sides of the trench. A profile drawing of this trench was made (Figure 5), and a moderate amount of excavated artifacts was removed from the trench fill. Artifacts from Trench 3 include 154 sherds, one piece of flaked stone, and one basalt shaft straightener (Figure 6a).

In addition to the house floors observed in Trenches 2 and 3, the Owens brothers reported that a cremation burial had been exposed a few years ago by road maintenance activities (grading) at the northern edge of Corona Road, at a point about 8 m north and 138 m east of datum. The burial and associated pottery were excavated and removed by the Owens's.

Artifact Assemblage

Using the sample and collection strategy described above, the field archaeologists recorded artifacts in 2030 1 m-by-1 m grid squares. Of these squares, 203 were designated for total collection of surface artifacts. A total of 201 sherds was collected from the 203 designated collection squares, but only 49 of these squares contained sherds. Similarly, 29 flaked stone artifacts (in 19 squares) and one ground stone artifact were collected.

Identification of all collected pottery was made by Bruce B. Huckell of the Arizona State Museum. The results of pottery identification sorting are shown in Table 1. The sample collection indicating that about three-fourths of the potsherds on the site surface are plain brown wares, and that the most common decorated type is Tanque Verde Red-on-brown. This type was made between A.D. 1200 and A.D. 1350 in the Tucson

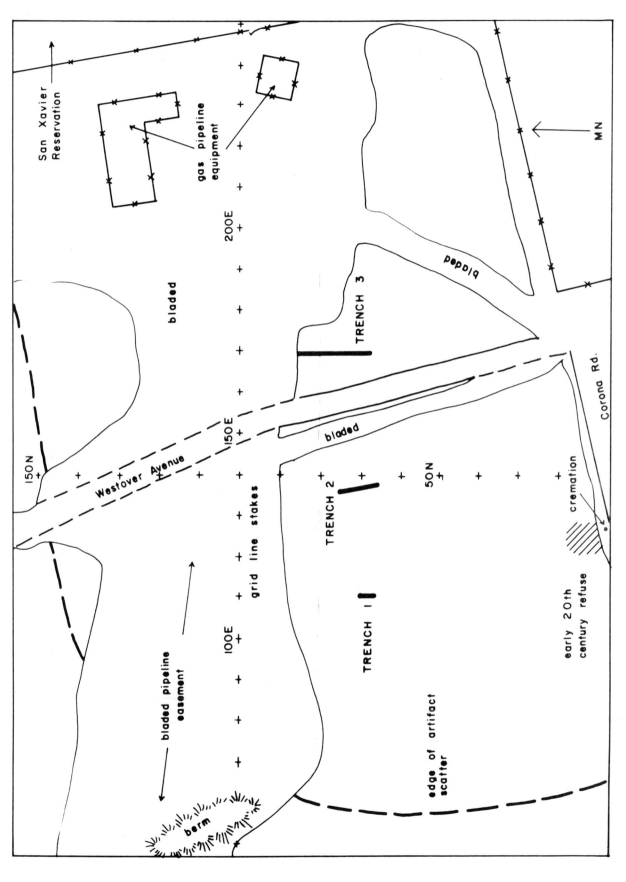

Figure 3. Site map of AZ AA:16:44

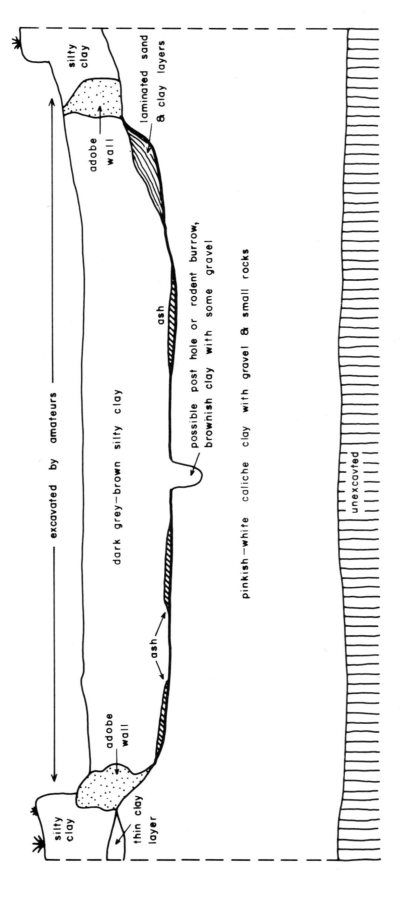

Figure 4. Profile of house in Trench 2 at AZ AA:16:44, looking west (1" = 40 cm)

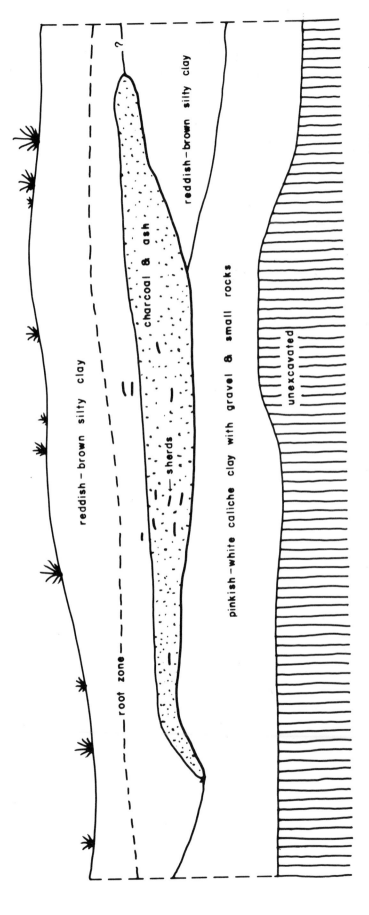

Figure 5. Floor profile of probable house in Trench 3 at AZ AA:16:44, looking east (1" = 40 cm)

Table 1. Pottery collected in 10-percent surface sample
AZ AA:16:44

Sample Unit*	Tanque Verde Red-on-brown	Rincon Red-on-brown	Unidentified Red-on-brown	Local Variant Sells Red	Unidentified Red	Plain Brown	Corrugated Brown	Total
90N 100E	-	-	-	-	-	3	-	3
30N 110E	1	-	1	-	-	3	-	5
40N 110E	1?	-	1	-	-	9	-	11
90N 120E	1	-	-	-	-	5	1	7
130N 120E	1	-	-	-	-	-	-	1
20N 130E	-	1	-	-	-	-	-	1
40N 130E	-	-	-	-	-	1	-	1
50N 130E	-	-	-	-	-	2	-	2
60N 130E	-	-	-	-	-	2	-	2
70N 130E	1?	-	-	-	-	2	-	3
80N 130E	1	-	1	-	-	4	-	6
30N 140E	-	-	1	-	-	2	-	3
90N 140E	-	-	-	-	-	5	-	5
100N 140E	-	-	1	-	-	3	-	4
30N 150E	1	-	-	-	-	2	-	3
40N 150E	1	-	-	-	-	2	-	3
30N 160E	1?	-	-	-	-	2	-	3
40N 160E	4	-	-	-	-	5	-	9
50N 160E	-	-	-	-	-	2	-	2
60N 160E	-	-	-	-	-	4	-	4
70N 160E	1?	-	-	-	-	3	-	4
20N 170E	-	-	-	-	-	1	-	1
30N 170E	-	-	-	-	-	1	-	1
40N 170E	-	-	-	-	-	1	-	1
70N 170E	-	-	-	-	-	1	-	1
80N 170E	-	-	2	-	-	4	-	6
90N 170E	-	-	1	-	-	2	-	3
30N 180E	1	-	-	-	-	2	-	3
40N 180E	-	-	-	1	-	2	-	3
50N 180E	-	-	-	-	-	1	-	1

*Only those sample units with sherds are listed.

Table 1. (continued)

Sample Unit*	Tanque Verde Red-on-brown	Rincon Red-on-brown	Unidentified Red-on-brown	Local Variant Sells	Unidentified Red	Plain Brown	Corrugated Brown	Total
60N 180E	-	-	-	-	-	1	-	1
70N 180E	-	-	-	-	-	3	-	3
60N 190E	2	-	2	-	1	8	-	13
70N 190E	-	-	-	-	-	3	-	3
70N 200E	-	-	-	-	-	3	-	3
80N 200E	3?	-	1	-	-	6	-	10
90N 200E	2	-	-	-	-	5	-	7
100N 200E	3	-	-	-	-	1	-	4
40N 210E	-	-	-	-	-	3	-	3
70N 220E	3	-	1	-	-	7	-	11
60N 230E	-	-	-	-	-	4	-	4
70N 230E	5	-	-	-	-	1	-	6
60N 240E	1?	-	-	-	-	3	-	4
70N 240E	-	-	-	-	-	3	-	3
50N 250E	-	-	-	-	-	9	-	9
60N 250E	-	-	1	-	-	7	-	8
70N 250E	-	-	-	-	-	3	-	3
50N 260E	-	-	1	-	-	2	-	3
70N 260E	-	-	-	-	-	1	-	1
Total	34	1	14	1	1	149	1	201
Percent	17.4	0.5	7.0	0.5	0.5	74.1	0.5	99.5

*Only those sample units with sherds are listed.

Basin. One sherd of Rincon Red-on-brown was identified in the sample
collection, and this type was manufactured somewhat earlier than Tanque
Verde Red-on-brown. The "Unidentified Red-on-brown" category in Table 1
consists of sherds with too little design present to identify as to type;
these might also be Tanque Verde or Rincon Red-on-brown, but this is
conjectural. All of the other pottery types identified in the 1-percent
sample collection are consistent in temporal placement with Tanque Verde
Red-on-brown, indicating human occupation beginning around A.D. 1200.

To determine if any types other than those in the 1-percent sample
could be identified, pottery was also collected at random from piles left
at the site by artifact collectors who had been digging there. Almost
all of the sherds collected in this way are Tanque Verde Red-on-brown or
plain wares, but two types not shown in the 1-percent sample (Table 1)
were also identified. These are Sells Red (same as the local variant
of Sells Red, but containing mica tempering material) and a White Mountain
Red Ware that is unidentifiable to specific type. Huckell says that both
of these wares are fairly common intrusives into Tucson Basin Classic
Hohokam sites.

Sherds collected from the test trenches are summarized in Table 2.
Trench 3 was the longest trench excavated, and so yielded the largest
quantity of artifacts. It probably went directly through a "burned house
area."

In addition to pottery sherds, other ceramic items from AZ
AA:16:44 were donated to the Arizona State Museum collection by John and
Randy Owens. These included the torso of a small human figurine (Figure
6b), two other figurine fragments, and six large, fragmentary, brown ware
beads that probably were used as spindle whorls (Figure 6c).

A moderate amount of flaked stone was observed during the
sampling procedure. In the 1-percent sample, 29 flaked stone items were
collected from 19 of the 203 squares designated for collection. Other
than a general correlation with high sherd density areas, no high concentration of lithics in particular areas was observed. Types of flaked
stone items in the sample include 24 flakes, three angular debris fragments, and two cores; data on these are summarized in Table 3. No formal
flaked stone tools were found during the testing project except a large
slate knife, possibly used in processing mescal hearths. Several
projectile points collected from the site were shown to the field
archaeologists by Randy Owens. Chert was the most common flaked stone
material observed, followed by basalt, quartzite, and petrified wood
(see Table 3). Very few of the samples observed were highly suitable to
flaking; 21 of the 29 collected items had cortex on their surfaces,
suggesting a paucity of available flintknapping materials.

Only two ground stone artifacts were collected, one from the
1-percent surface sample and the other from Trench 3. In the 1-percent
sample collection is a quartzite two-hand mano fragment found at 80N 130E

Table 2. Pottery collected from backhoe trenches at AZ AA:16:44

Location	Number and Types of Sherds
Trench 1, fill	1 Sells Red
	4 plain brown
Trench 2, fill	3 Tanque Verde Red-on-brown
	8 plain brown
Trench 3, fill	36 Tanque Verde Red-on-brown
	5 probable Tanque Verde Red-on-brown
	2 unidentified Red-on-brown
	5 local variant of Sells Red
	92 plain brown (1 intentionally broken to form disk)
Trench 3, east face profile	3 Tanque Verde Red-on-brown (1 broken to form disk)
	11 plain brown

Table 3. Flaked stone items collected in 10-percent surface sample at AZ AA:16:44

	Flakes				Angular Debris		Cores	
	Utilized		Unutilized					
Material	With Cortex	No Cortex	With Cortex	No Cortex	With Cortex	No Cortex	With Cortex	No Cortex
Chert	6	5	7	1	2	-	1	-
Basalt	-	1	2	-	-	-	1	-
Quartzite	1	-	-	1	-	-	-	-
Petrified Wood	-	-	-	-	1	-	-	-

of datum. The other item is a basalt shaft straightener (Figure 6a) with
a single groove and a raised projection suitable for bending wooden shafts
out straight. Four other pieces of ground stone were observed in the
10-percent surface observation sample. In addition to these, Randy Owens
showed the field archaeologists two basalt ax heads that he recovered from
the site. One of the axes is from the cremation burial excavated by the
Owens's.

Six pieces of worked shell items from AZ AA:16:44 were donated to
the site collection by John and Randy Owens. These included fragments of
two bracelets (Figure 6d), two rings, a carved frog figurine (Figure 6e),
and one Conus shell tinkler.

In addition to prehistoric items at AZ AA:16:44, several scatters
of historic refuse were observed. Most of these appear to be quite recent,
dating after 1950. One scatter, however, is notably older, probably
dating to the early 20th century. This scatter was found adjacent to
Corona Road (Figure 3) and consists of several sherds of ironstone
pottery; steel can fragments; aqua, amethyst, and opalescent glass fragments; and some sawed mammal bones. Some of the glassware in this scatter
was manufactured prior to World War I, suggesting that the scatter predates
1920. Elsewhere on the site, in the bladed gas pipeline easement, a few
brown ware sherds with clear glaze were recorded; these are probably of
a recent Mexican ware. Other scatters of sawed mammal bones were also
observed in various places on the site.

Conclusions

A Classic Period Hohokam occupation of the Tanque Verde Phase is
indicated by the artifacts observed and collected from AZ AA:16:44. In
addition, the site was used historically, in the early 20th century,
probably as a temporary campsite, and has been used repeatedly in the past
few decades for discarding unwanted materials, routing gas pipelines, and
collecting Indian artifacts.

The most commonly found artifacts during the archaeological testing program were broken potsherds, with lesser amounts of flaked and
ground stone. The remains of two prehistoric house floors observed in the
test excavations indicate that the site was used for habitation, and the
large quantity of surface litter plus the depth of cultural deposit (as
much as 40 cm), suggests a long-term occupation. Finely crafted items
such as shell jewelry, decorated pottery, and polished stone axes indicate
a highly developed crafts industry among the prehistoric inhabitants of
the site. Information from local artifact collectors suggests that AZ
AA:16:44 has seen relatively little subsurface disturbance except for the
laying of a subsurface gas pipeline and a few amateur archaeological
excavations.

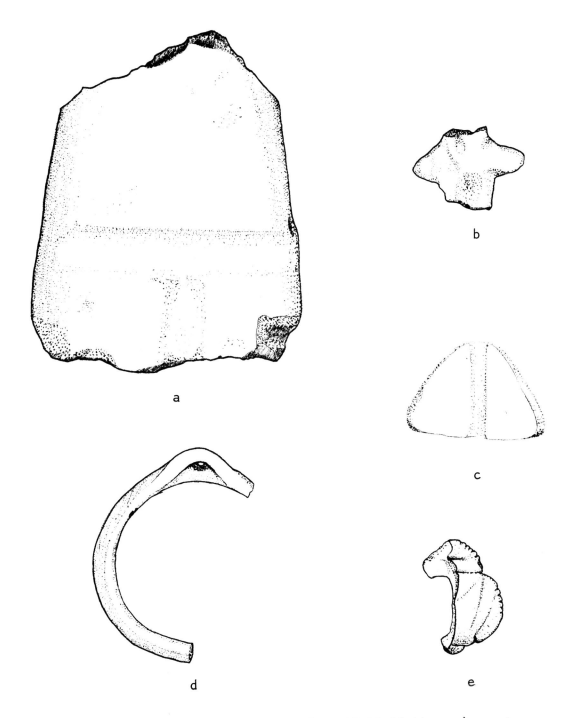

Figure 6. Miscellaneous artifacts from AZ AA:16:44 a) basalt
shaft straightener; b) human figurine torso; c) brown ware spindle
whorl; d) shell bracelet fragment; e) carved frog figurine. Shaft
straightener (6a) from Trench 3; 6b-e from collection of John and
Randy Owens.

Recommendations

Judging from the amount of prehistoric trash and the depth of cultural materials, AZ AA:16:44 has significant potential for a study of former lifeways and social organization of the Tucson Basin Hohokam Indians of the Tanque Verde Phase, and for comparison with more distant Hohokam groups such as those in the Casa Grande and Snaketown areas. Because of this research potential, as well as the possible contribution to our knowledge of the area's land use patterns in the late 19th and early 20th centuries, the site is significant. It is likely to yield important information about prehistory and history in the Tucson Basin. The Arizona State Museum recommends a program of scientific mitigation of the damage that would be caused by the construction of a housing development at the site. Such a program should include carefully controlled archaeological excavation of the portion of the site that will be affected by construction activities, done in the context of scientific research proposals developed specifically for this site. The program should also include time and facilities for analyses and interpretations of all recovered data. The compilation of a photographic record of items collected from the site by John and Randy Owens is also encouraged, and this record should include all provenience data available from these amateur archaeologists. A final report on the mitigation program should be prepared for distribution to the scientific community, so that the information on AZ AA:16:44 can be put to use in studies of the prehistoric past.

If such a program of data recovery is carried out, then the housing project proposed by Pulte Home Corporation should have no adverse effect on cultural resources. Archaeological clearance can be recommended once field archaeological investigations have been completed.

Acknowledgments

The assistance of Pulte Home Corporation in making available a backhoe and operator to the field archaeologists is gratefully acknowledged. Also, the small collection of artifacts donated to the Arizona State Museum by John and Randy Owens, and their comments on the site, are greatly appreciated.

CHAPTER 3

ARCHAEOLOGICAL COLLECTION AND TESTING AT AZ EE:7:22,
A SITE IN THE BABOCOMARI VALLEY, COCHISE COUNTY, ARIZONA

by

Allen Dart

with contributions by

Charles H. Miksicek
Suzanne K. Fish

for

City of Huachuca City, Arizona

The Cultural Resource Management Division
Arizona State Museum
University of Arizona

October 1980

Table of Contents

List of Figures

List of Tables

Abstract

Archaeological subsurface testing and collection of artifacts were conducted at AZ EE:7:22, a small site containing prehistoric pottery, stone artifacts, and a roasting pit feature, along with two historic land alterations. An analysis of all artifacts, and of botanical samples collected from the roasting pit, suggests that the site was occupied temporarily at least twice, and was used primarily for processing of wild food resources. The project was done to determine whether archaeological clearance could be recommended for the area, which is the proposed site of a wastewater treatment facility. Due to the lack of extensive subsurface remains, and because all observed artifacts were collected, the Arizona State Museum recommended clearance for the proposed project construction.

Acknowledgments

Special thanks are extended to Terry McGriff, City Clerk of Huachuca City, for arranging military clearance for the testing involved in this project, as well as making a backhoe available. Mayor Bob Fenimore's help is also gratefully acknowledged. The following folks operated the backhoe: Art Ostrander, Dave Moore, Pete Herring, and Don Alsvick. Their forbearance on a not-too-interesting job is appreciated.

We are grateful to Lt. Col. Claude D. Boyd and Ft. Huachuca Real Estate Officer Frank Hedgcock, for giving us access to the restricted military land on which the project was carried out. Their concern for the safety of the crew was shown by their insistence that the project area be inspected for, and cleared of, any leftover ordnance materials from former military maneuvers in the area.

Charles Miksicek analyzed the flotation samples, and Suzanne K. Fish the pollen samples, which were taken from a roasting pit found at the site. They both had to make time for these analyses while doing work for another archaeological project, and their willingness to do so helped us immensely in generating an informative report. Likewise, the aid of Bruce B. Huckell in identifying pottery types recovered from the site, as well as his helpful suggestions regarding literature sources, is appreciated. Finally, Susan A. Brew is acknowledged for directing the project and for incorporating biological sample analysis results into this report, and Ron Gardiner is recognized for his excellent fieldwork.

Introduction

On August 26 and September 24-25, 1980, Arizona State Museum archaeologists Ron Gardiner and Allen Dart conducted an archaeological testing and artifact collection program at AZ EE:7:22, an archaeological site consisting of prehistoric pottery and flaked stone concentrations, one partial roasting pit, and two fairly recent bulldozer-disturbed areas. The goal of the program was to determine the nature and distribution of surface artifacts, the depth of cultural materials, and the nature and depth of any architectural features. The site's future research potential, significance, and eligibility for inclusion on the National Register of Historic Places were also assessed.

An inspection for archaeological remains had been conducted in June, 1980, for Huachuca City by Arizona State Museum archaeologist Earl W. Sires. The survey area included approximately 20 acres of land that is the proposed site of an additional wastewater treatment facility. During the initial archaeological inspection, AZ EE:7:22 was recorded, and additional work to further evaluate this cultural resource was recommended. Mr. Terry McGriff, City Clerk for Huachuca City, authorized the Arizona State Museum to conduct this additional work, which included recording of surface artifacts and features, subsurface excavations, and analysis of artifacts and biological samples collected from the site, on behalf of Huachuca City's City Council.

Physical Setting

AZ EE:7:22 is located east of the town of Huachuca City, Arizona, in the SE 1/4 of the NW 1/4 of Section 33, T20S, R20E, on the floodplain of the Babocomari River (Figure 1). The site is situated along both sides of a deeply dissected arroyo which drains northeastward into the Babocomari, in a vegetation association of mesquite, some catclaw acacia, and various grasses. Tumbleweeds are growing in areas disturbed recently by roads and notably in two depressions evidently produced by a bulldozer. Much of the site area surrounding the arroyo is sheetwashing into the arroyo, leaving the ground barren (Figure 2).

Methodology

Field archaeologists made a visual inspection of the project area to determine the extent of surface artifacts, then a site map was made using an alidade, plane table, and stadia rod (Figure 3). Modern reference points such as fences, roads, and the arroyo were plotted on

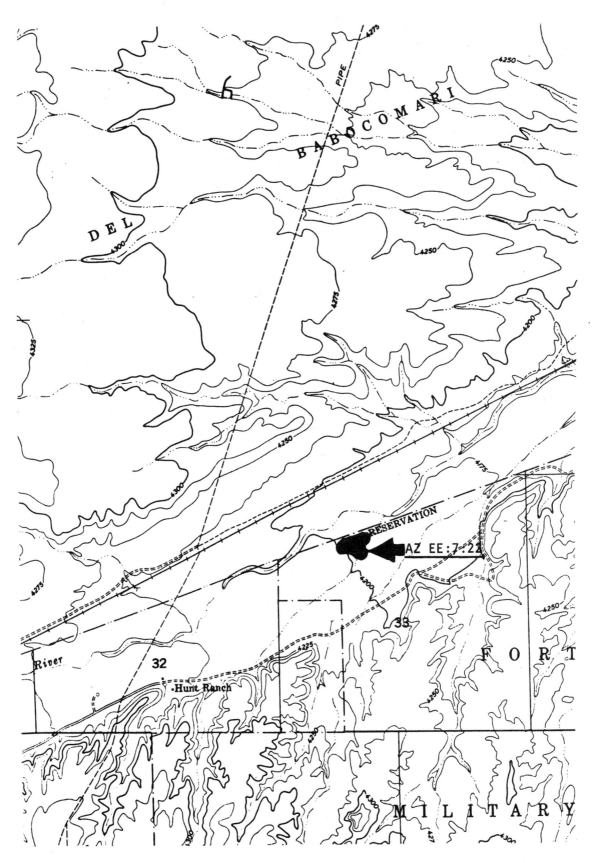

Figure 1. Location of AZ EE:7:22

Figure 2. View of AZ EE:7:22,
looking southeast

this map. After pinflagging surface artifacts or artifact clusters, the
main areas of artifact concentrations were sketched onto the map, along
with a prehistoric roasting pit found eroding out in the arroyo bank.

After the locations of the surface artifact concentrations had
been determined, all observed artifacts were collected, with artifacts
from each concentration being bagged separately. Next, backhoe trenches
were excavated in various areas to determine whether any subsurface artifacts or architectural features might be present. A total of ten trenches
were dug; seven of these were in areas of highest artifact density, two
in areas of low artifact density, and one in one of the bulldozer-made
features (Figure 3). After excavation, the faces of each trench were
examined to detect the presence of architectural features and to determine the depth of cultural deposits. All artifacts found during
excavation were collected. Profile drawings were made of several
trenches. Of the profiled trenches, only Trench 3 showed signs of man-
made disturbance. All trenches were backfilled after study was
completed.

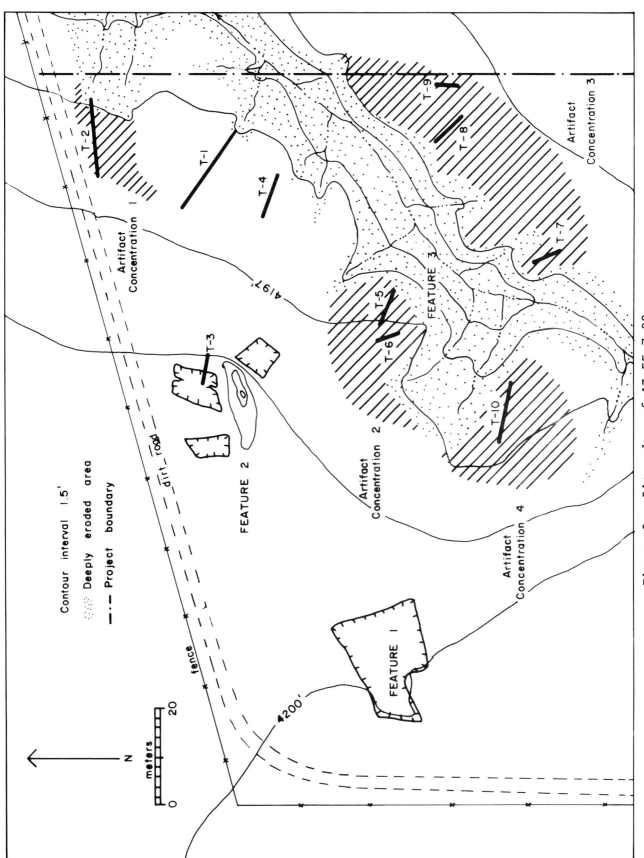

Figure 3. Site plan of AZ EE:7:22

Artifact and Features Distribution

Four artifact concentrations were observable. They were separated from one another by the arroyo or by an area of much lower artifact density. Each of the concentrations was assigned a number (Figure 3), and all the artifacts within each concentration were collected. A light scatter of artifacts between Artifact Concentrations 1 and 2 was collected separately from either of these concentrations.

Three man-made features were found at the site in addition to the fences and dirt roads. Features 1 and 2 are evidently the result of 20th century bulldozer activities. Feature 1 is an L-shaped depression measuring about 32 m by 23 m in its maximum extent, and 0.40 m deep. It is about 30 m away from the nearest artifact concentration. Feature 2 consists of an oblong dirt mound about a meter high, amid three, four-sided depressions which are a maximum of 14 m by 8 m in extent; the whole feature measures about 35 m in diameter. Feature 2 is about 50 m east of Feature 1, and about 10 m north of Artifact Concentration 2.

The third feature was observed eroding out in the arroyo bank, at the edge of Artifact Concentration 2. It was a small roasting pit partially filled with charcoal, ash, and fire-cracked rocks. Its bottom was only 17 cm below the present ground surface. This features is illustrated in Figures 4 and 5.

Excavations

Table 1 is a summary of the locations of backhoe test trenches with respect to artifact and feature locations, and the artifacts removed from each. As can be seen from the table, only three trenches yielded any artifacts, and none showed evidence of architectural features.

In addition to the backhoe excavations, the roasting pit (Feature 3) was hand-excavated by Ron Gardiner. All dirt and ash within the pit was saved for flotation analysis of vegetal remains and for pollen identification. The surrounding surface within 1 m of the pit was troweled down to see if there was any evidence of an associated occupation surface. Nothing was found to indicate an associated surface, nor were there any artifacts associated with the pit.

Artifact Assemblage

Artifact types found at AZ EE:7:22 include pottery sherds, flaked stone tools and flakes, and ground stone. Each of these is discussed separately below.

Table 1. Test trenches at AZ EE:7:22

Trench Number	Location	Subsurface Artifacts	Evidence of Features
1	Between A.C. 1 and 2	1 sherd	None
2	Within A.C. 1	3 sherds	None
3	Within Feature 2	None	Profile of bulldozer cut
4	Between A.C. 1 and 2	None	None
5	Within A.C. 2	None	None
6	Within A.C. 2	None	None
7	Within SW portion of A.C. 3	None	None
8	Within NE portion of A.C. 3	None	None
9	Within NE portion of A.C. 3	None	None
10	Within A.C. 4	2 sherds, 1 flake	None

A.C. = Artifact Concentration

Pottery

Pottery type identifications were made by Bruce B. Huckell of the Arizona State Museum. In general, he is of the impression that the decorated sherds from AZ EE:7:22 are Tucson Basin Hohokam wares which exhibit considerable Mogollon influence. Several of the plain ware sherds show an affinity to San Francisco Red pottery of the Mogollon region of southeastern Arizona and southwestern New Mexico, being well finished with a slight reddish color, but lacking a good polish.

A total of 394 sherds was collected from the site; an over-whelming majority of these, 96.4%, are plain wares (Table 2), and the distribution of the few decorated sherds is biased entirely towards the northwest side of the arroyo. The 14 decorated sherds are almost evenly divided among Artifact Concentrations 2 and 4, and the sparser group

Table 2. Pottery collected from AZ EE:7:22

Field Specimen Number and Location On Site	Plain	Unidentified Red-on-brown	Rillito Red-on-brown	Encinas Red-on-brown	Gila Butte Red-on-buff	Dragoon Red Ware	Total	Percent
1 (A.C. 1)	44 (98%)	1 (2%)	-	-	-	-	45	11.4
4 (Between A.C. 1 and 2)	30 (83%)	5 (14%)	-	-	-	1 (3%)	36	9.1
5 (A.C. 2)	98 (96%)	4 (4%)	-	-	-	-	102	25.9
8 (A.C. 4)	93 (97%)	-	1 (1%)	1 (1%)	1 (1%)	-	96	24.4
9 (A.C. 3)	109	-	-	-	-	-	109	27.7
11 (A.C. 4, Trench 10)	2	-	-	-	-	-	2	0.5
13 (Between A.C. 1 and 2, T-1)	1	-	-	-	-	-	1	0.3
14 (A.C. 1, T-2)	3	-	-	-	-	-	3	0.7
Total	380	10	1	1	1	1	394	100.0
Percent	96.4	2.5	0.3	0.3	0.3	0.3	100.1	

A.C. = Artifact Concentration

of sherds between Artifact Concentrations 1 and 2. Decorated types identified by Huckell were Rillito Red-on-brown, Encinas Red-on-brown, Gila Butte Red-on-buff, and a "Dragoon" series red ware (Fulton 1934:7, 14) with one example of each. Also, 10 red-on-brown sherds were found that could not be identified as to specific type because of their small size.

An attempt was made to estimate the relative numbers of pottery jars to bowls, based on rim forms among the plain ware sherds and on which side the design was painted on decorated sherds. This information is summarized in Table 3. Since the boundaries between the separate artifact concentrations do not preclude the possibility that sherds from one vessel might be scattered among two or more proveniences, an estimate of jars versus bowls for each provenience was not attempted. In fact, some of the rim sherds from separate concentrations look as if they may have been from single vessels. Table 3, then, summarizes jars versus bowls for the entire site collection, and the numbers represent the minimum number of vessels of each form present. Only distinctly different rim forms or pottery types were considered separate vessels. The summary suggests that there are almost twice as many jars as bowls.

Table 3. Minimum numbers of jars and bowls at AZ EE:7:22

Jars, decorated wares	2	
Jars, undecorated wares	5	Minimum number of jars 7

- -

Bowls, decorated wares	2	
Bowls, undecorated wares	5	Minimum number of bowls 4

Lithic Artifacts

The analysis of the lithic artifact assemblage from AZ EE:7:22 followed the approach of Bayham (1976). Bayham has suggested that edge damage on stone items which is visible to the naked eye is an indication of prehistoric use, and that the angle of the damaged or "working" edge may be a key to the item's function. Following Wilmsen (1970:79) and Gould and others (1971:151), Bayham (1976:109, 117) states, "Relatively steep edge angles...[between 35 degrees and 70 degrees] have frequently been associated with heavy wood cutting and wood working." He also proposes that flakes used in simple evisceration of rabbits would generally have an edge angle of 35 degrees of less.

Table 4. Types of lithic artifacts, numbers with macroscopic edge damage, and mean edge angles of those with macroscopic edge damage

	Specimen Number and Location						Total
	2 (A.C. 1)	3 (Between A.C. 1 and 2)	6 (A.C. 2)	7 (A.C. 4)	10 (A.C. 3)	12 (A.C. 4)	
Cores	3	1	3	-	2	-	9
Edge-damaged	2	1	1	-	2	-	6
Mean edge angle	50°	50°	71°		84°		65°
Flakes	18	4	24	15	15	1	77
Edge-damaged	9	4	8	6	12*	1	40
Mean edge angle	41°	31°	35°	37°	54°	30°	41°
Non-flakes	2	-	1	3	3	-	9
Edge-damaged	-	-	-	1	1	-	2
Mean edge angle				36°	49°		43°
Mano	-	-	-	-	1	-	1
Total	23	5	28	18	21	1	96

*One flake damaged on two edges; both angles were measured and counted separately.

Note: A.C. = Artifact Concentration

In order to help ascertain site functions, the edge angles and forms of stone artifacts showing edge damage were monitored. Material types were also noted to provide insight into the availability of stone materials to the site's inhabitants. This analysis is presented in Table 4. The categories "core," "flake," and "non-flake" follow the definition of Bayham (1976:197). Three lithic artifacts did not fit into these categories: one mano fragment was found in Artifact Concentration 3, and Artifact Concentration 2 and Artifact Concentration 4 each contained one fire-cracked cobble.

Of a total of 96 stone artifacts collected at AZ EE:7:22, nine were cores, and six of these showed damaged edges averaging 65 degrees. Range of edge angles on edge-damaged cores was 48 degrees to 86 degrees. The high edge angle average of the utilized cores may suggest that they were indeed used for wood processing activities, as Bayham suggested.

Seventy-seven of the lithic artifacts were flakes; of these, 40 showed macroscopic edge damage. Edge angles on the edge-damaged flakes ranged from 17 degrees to 90 degrees, with 41 degrees the average. This indicates they were not used as evisceration tools. It is interesting to note, however, that Artifact Concentration 2 and Artifact Concentration 4, and zones between Artifact Concentration 1 and Artifact Concentration 2, had damaged flakes with average angles of 35 degrees or less. This suggests that gutting activities occurred in these areas. In fact, there was a wide range of measurements within each artifact concentration, so it is likely that several activities, possibly including both woodworking and animal evisceration, were occurring.

Artifact Concentration 3 was unique because of the steeply angled edges of both utilized cores and flakes recovered there. The steep angles of the flakes may be accounted for, at least partially, by the fact that seven of them had concave working edges averaging 58 degrees, suggesting "spoke-shave" or shaft-scraping activities.

Nine non-flakes were recovered. Of these, only two showed evident edge damage, and both had moderate working edge angles.

The stone material most commonly utilized at AZ EE:7:22 was basalt (Table 5). All the basalt observed was fairly fine-ground, and it ranged in color from a dark gray to a dark gray lavender. Quartzite was the second most prevalent material, and there were lesser amounts of rhyolite, chert, limestone, and slate. The mano found in Artifact Concentration 3 is of sandstone. The stone materials selected at AZ EE:7:22 contrast sharply with those DiPeso (1951:130-187) reported at the Babocomari Village site (AZ EE:7:1), located about four miles upstream along the Babocomari River from AZ EE:7:22. At the Babocomari Village, DiPeso reported no basalt present, although the other stone types found at AZ EE:7:22 were also found at the Village site. This might be the result of different overall activities going on at each site; for example, habitation and processing of agricultural products at the Village site as opposed to,

Table 5. Lithic materials utilized at AZ EE:7:22

	Basalt	Quartz-ite	Rhyo-lite	Chert	Lime-stone	Slate	Sand-stone
Number of Items	61	20	8	3	2	1	1
Percent of Total	63.5%	20.8%	8.3%	3.1%	2.1%	1.0%	1.0%

perhaps, temporary camping and wild food processing at AZ EE:7:22. Other possible reasons for the differences could be the different periods of occupation at each site: between A.D. 900 and 1200 at AZ EE:7:22, A.D. 1200-1450 at Babocomari Village (DiPeso 1951:239); or that AZ EE:7:22 may simply have been close to an accessible source of basalt.

Botanical Analysis of Feature 3

All the dirt, charcoal, and ash confined in Feature 3 (the roasting pit) was collected for flotation and pollen analyses. The layer above the rocks in this feature was kept separate from the layer of fill below the rocks (Figure 4). The rocks themselves were discarded in the field. Flotation analysis was done by Charles H. Miksicek, and pollen analysis by Suzanne K. Fish, both of the Arizona State Museum. Reports on their findings follow.

Flotation Analysis at AZ EE:7:22

by Charles H. Miksicek

Flotation analysis of two samples collected from Feature 3, a roasting pit, revealed the following plant and snail remains:

Sample 2--Above Layer of Rocks (7.0 gms of floated material)

7 fragments of Fourwing Saltbush wood charcoal (Atriplex canescens)
5 Hawaiia miniscula snails

Sample 1--Below Layer of Rocks (3.0 gms of floated material)

4 fragments of Saltbush charcoal
3 fragments of Cholla buds (Opuntia sp.)
2 Hawaiia miniscula snails
1 Hydrobiidae snail
1 Pupoides albilabris snail

All of the snail types are dry-land snails, usually native to higher elevations in the Southwest (up to the Transition Life Zone, 7000+ feet), but the published literature is not very specific about lower range limits. They inhabit moist, rocky areas with abundant leaf litter. In all likelihood, they are post-depositional intrusions, small snails that found a favorable habitat in moist mesquite leaf litter among the rocks of Feature 3.

The cholla buds were fragmentary parenchymous material. In terms of micro-anatomy, these fragments compared favorably to modern, dried and carbonized Opuntia versicolor buds. In all likelihood, Feature 3 was a cholla roasting pit, suggesting that the site itself was a seasonally used cholla collecting camp.

Ethnographically, small pits were dug for roasting cholla buds. A mesquite fire was built in the pit for the purpose of heating rocks. After the fire burned down, the ashes, coals, and rocks were removed from the pit. A layer of Suaeda torreyana (Inkweed or Quelite-salado) was then placed in the pit and covered with cholla buds. More inkweed was then placed over the buds and hot rocks were shoveled into the pit. More layers of inkweed, cholla buds, and hot rocks were added to this and the whole pit was covered with earth. After 24 hours of steaming the pit was opened up and the cholla buds were removed and sun-dried for storage. Prepared and dried this way, cholla buds would keep for a number of years. Before cooking and eating, the cholla buds would be rehydrated by soaking in water (Castetter and Underhill, 1935).

Suaeda and Atriplex are close relatives, both members of the Chenopodiaceae (Goosefoot Family). Both plants are halophytes, but Suaeda tolerates soils with higher salinity. The nearest large stands of Suaeda to Huachuca City are on the Wilcox Playa where it is the only plant species that can survive the high salt levels near the center of the dry lake bed. Apparently the prehistoric people who constructed Feature 3 substituted Atriplex for Suaeda, probably because of greater local availability. Saltbush produces a very hot fire and its leaves and small stems would have served the same purpose as Suaeda leaves. In addition the ashes of saltbush could have been used as a salt substitute.

Unless other plant species in the area were exploited at different times, AZ EE:7:22 was probably occupied between early April and early May, just before the local species of cholla burst into full bloom.

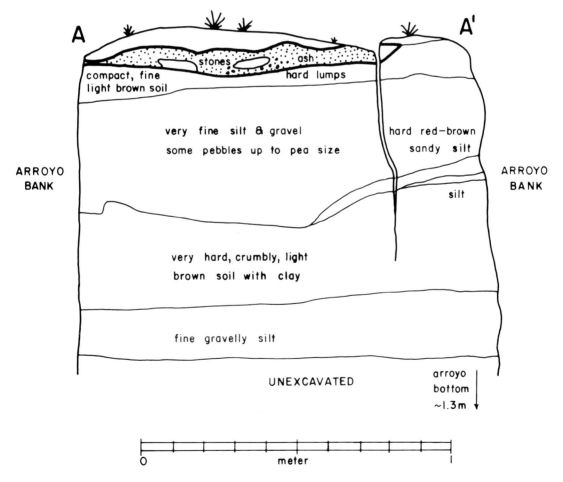

Figure 4.   Feature 3 (roasting pit) as seen in profile, looking north

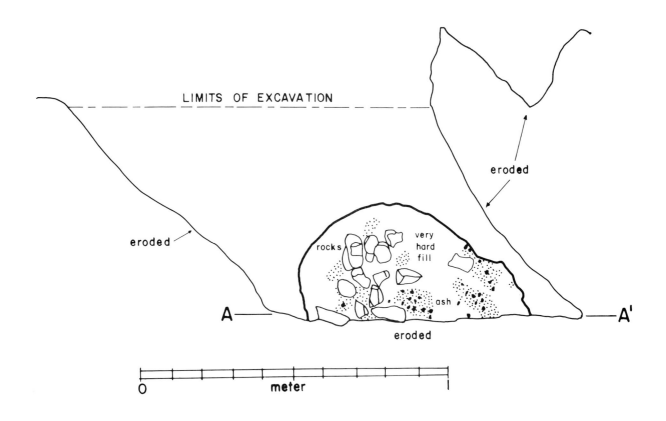

Figure 5. Feature 3 (roasting pit) during excavation

Pollen Analysis at AZ EE:7:22

by Suzanne K. Fish

Two pollen samples were analyzed from Feature 3, a roasting pit.
One was collected above rocks in the fill in the upper part of the pit,
and one was collected below them. Both samples appear to indicate an
open landscape, with grass and herbaceous types of pollen dominating the
record. Arboreal types include pine and oak in low quantities. The
frequencies probably indicate wind-blown pollen intrusions from vegetation
at some distance. More immediate arboreal types are represented by one
grain each of acacia, mimosa, mesquite, and palo-verde pollen. These
taxa produce little pollen, so that presence in the pollen record is
likely to indicate occurrence in the general vicinity. Relative quantity
cannot be inferred, however.

Cheno-Am pollen, composed of pollen of Chenopodiaceae and the
genus Amaranthus was the most numerous type in both samples. The lower
sample had the higher frequency at 51 percent, compared with 37.5 percent
in the other. This pollen type occurred in aggregates in both samples.
Since aggregates of pollen are heavy and would not be distributed by
wind, direct presence of plant parts is indicated. Atriplex, or saltbush, was recovered in the flotation remains. It is likely that the
abundance of Cheno-Am pollen is another indication of use of this plant
in the pit.

Yucca pollen also was encountered in aggregates; none was
observed as single grains. Yucca buds, fruits, and flower stalks have
been eaten by Southwestern groups. The presence of pollen is more
likely to be associated with this use than with use of the yucca leaf
fibers or roots. Yucca pollen was found only in the upper sample.

Several yucca species are known to occur in Cochise County in
environments similar to AZ EE:7:22 (Kearney and Peebles 1964:187-88).
Combined flowering seasons of these species begins in April and ends in
August. Pollen persisting on the plant after the flowering season might
add to the end date of probable introduction of pollen into a site.

Conclusions

AZ EE:7:22 appears to have been occupied temporarily on one or
more occasions, judging from decorated pottery types which were identified. The Gila Butte Red-on-buff type has been associated with the Gila
Butte Phase of the Gila Basin, dated by archaeologists to A.D. 700-900
(Kelly and others 1978:4). The Rillito Red-on-brown type occurs in the
Rillito Phase of the Tucson Basin, and has been associated with the
Santa Cruz Phase at the Gila Basin, dated to A.D. 700-900 (Kelly and
others 1978:4). The Encinas Red-on-brown type is poorly documented, but
by association with other types of pottery which have been dated by

tree-ring methods (Three Circle Neck Corrugated, Forestdale Smudged, San Francisco Red, Mimbres Classic, and Mimbres Bold Face Black-on-white) to between A.D. 750 and 1347, it is conceivable that it might have been deposited some time between A.D. 700 and 800, as the other two might have been. Therefore, if only a single occupation period occurred, it was probably during the middle of the 8th century. The wide temporal span of the pottery dates, however, indicates three or more separate occupations at the site.

The physical setting of AZ EE:7:22, that is, the floodplain of the Babocomari River, suggests it was a site selected for occupation because of its proximity to both water and wild food resources. DiPeso (1951:2-8) documents the physical changes which are known to have occurred in the Babocomari Valley since early historic times. He notes that the river still flowed as late as 1878, that large cienegas existed in places, and that there were abundant nutritional grasses on the pediment flats above the valley. The heavy growths of mesquite which presently characterize the floodplain evidently did not take hold until after 1910, when Anglo farmers were forced to move out of the valley by a court decision. His data suggest that, during prehistoric times, the river and its tributary streams were not entrenched as they are today, and that running water was available.

The analysis of the site artifacts suggests that AZ EE:7:22 was used only seasonally, for gathering and processing wild plant food products. The artifact assemblage shows that there probably were a greater number of pottery jars than bowls present, and that plain wares far outnumbered decorated wares. Only one piece of ground stone was observed; some of the other stone artifacts appear to have been used for woodworking, but the majority of them, especially flakes, have sharper edge angles suggestive of nonwoodworking activities. And finally, a rock-filled roasting pit was found at the site.

What can we deduce from this assemblage? Probably our best clue to site activities is the roasting pit and its contents. Similar roasting pits have been found on other archaeological projects in southern and central Arizona. Ethnographic research was conducted to determine their use (Goodyear 1975; Doelle 1976). From ethnographic studies and literature on the historic Pima and Papago, it was concluded that these roasting pits were used primarily for processing the flower buds of cholla cactus, a food resource which became available in early spring, especially May, when few other wild plant resources and no agricultural products were available (Goodyear 1975:63-66; Doelle 1976:78-79). Analysis of the carbonized plant remains from Feature 3 at AZ EE:7:22 supports this conclusion and indicates that one of the activities occurring at the site was the processing of cholla buds for food.

Artifacts used by historic Pima and Papago Indians in collecting and processing cholla buds were primarily wooden tongs to pluck the buds from the plant, and baskets to hold the collected buds, and neither of these could be expected at an exposed archaeological site (Goodyear

1975:66). However, a number of stone artifacts at AZ EE:7:22 with relatively steep working edge angles, especially those with concave working edges, suggest woodworking activities for collecting cactus buds. Goodyear (1975:66) also notes that large numbers of ceramics would not necessarily be associated with cholla bud processing sites, nor would ground stone be expected. If this is true, then other activities besides pit-baking of cholla buds may have occurred at AZ EE:7:22, since one mano and numerous ceramics were found.

Doelle (1976:78-79) notes that cholla cactus buds can be processed for human consumption by either pit-baking or boiling, and that boiling is more efficient in terms of labor needed, provided water is available. It is possible, then, that the large number of pottery vessels present at the site indicate that cholla buds were also being processed by boiling.

Castetter and Bell describe ethnographic use of both yucca fruit and buds by Papago and Apache Indians. They report (1941:15-16, 19) that partially ripened yucca fruits were collected, placed on beds of dry grass, and covered with another layer of grass to complete their ripening. Then the fruits were removed and split open. The seed ribbons were withdrawn, and the ripe fruit halves dried in the sun. This dried fruit could be pulverized and eaten as gruel. Yucca processing at AZ EE:7:22 may then explain the presence of the mano. It was further mentioned that the large flowers of Yucca elata were boiled and eaten as a vegetable, and the yucca crowns were gathered any time from the middle of March until the end of summer and the portion of the stem between the ground and the leaves was peeled and baked overnight. The baked product was then dried in the sun, and later softened in water and eaten. It is also possible, then, that the large number of pottery vessels present at the site can be attributed to the boiling and soaking of yucca plant parts during processing.

We may suggest, then, that AZ EE:7:22 was used temporarily for more than one type of wild food gathering activity, and that it was occupied during at least two separate periods of the year. If cholla buds were processed there, as it appears they were, this activity would have occurred during springtime, probably in May. Yucca was probably collected and utilized between April and August. If more than one season's use is represented, this lends support to the idea that the different pottery types present may indicate two or more occupation periods which were separated in time by as much as 200 years or more. It is possible, also, that some exploitation of animals for food was occurring at the site, although the only suggestion of this is a number of stone flakes with small-angle (35 degrees or less) working edges.

Recommendations

In a total of 10 backhoe trenches on the site, most in areas of relatively high artifact density, there were only eight potsherds and flakes removed from below the surface. There was no evidence found for subsurface architectural features except the single roasting pit (Feature 3) and the two obviously bulldozer-made features. All artifacts observed at the site were collected and analyzed, and the single roasting pit was excavated, recorded with drawings and photographs, and its contents sampled biologically. The artifact collection and site records are stored at the Arizona State Museum and are available for further research. The site itself appears unlikely to yield further information important in history or prehistory and, as such, we believe that construction of the proposed water treatment facility in the proposed project area will have no adverse effect on cultural resources. The Arizona State Museum therefore recommends archaeological clearance for the proposed project.

References

Bayham, Frank E.
   1976   Wood procurement; Faunal exploitation, Appendix II: Lithics.
             In "Desert Resources and Hohokam Subsistence: The CONOCO
             Florence Project," edited by William Harper Doelle. Arizona
             State Museum Archaeological Series 103:107-121; 195-217.
             Tucson: University of Arizona.

Bell, Willis H. and Edward F. Castetter
   1941   The utilization of yucca, sotol, and beargrass by the
             aborigines in the American Southwest. Ethnobiological
             studies in the American Southwest. The University of New
             Mexico Bulletin 5(5).

Breternitz, David A.
   1966   An appraisal of tree-ring dated pottery in the Southwest.
             Anthropological Papers of the University of Arizona 10. Tucson:
             University of Arizona Press.

DiPeso, Charles C.
   1951   The Babocomari Village site on the Babocomari River, south-
             eastern Arizona. Amerind Foundation, Inc. 5.

Doelle, William Harper
   1976   Desert resources and Hohokam subsistence: The CONOCO Florence
             project. Arizona State Museum Archaeological Series 103.
             Tucson: University of Arizona.

Fulton, William Shirley
   1934   Archaeological notes on Texas Canyon, Arizona. Contributions
             from the Museum of the American Indian, Heye Foundation 12(2).

Goodyear, Albert C.
   1975   Hecla II and III: An interpretive study of archaeological
             remains from the Lakeshore Project, Papago Reservation, south
             central Arizona. Arizona State University Anthropological
             Research Paper 9. Tempe: Arizona State University.

Gould, Richard A., D. A. Koster, and A. H. Sontz
   1971   The lithic assemblage of the Western Desert aborigines of
             Australia. American Antiquity 36(2):149-169.

Kearney, T. H. and R. H. Peebles
   1964   Arizona Flora. Berkeley: University of California Press.

Sayles, E. B.
    1945   The San Simon branch: Excavations at Cave Creek and in the
              San Simon Valley; I. Material Culture. Medallion Papers 34,
              Globe, Arizona: Gila Pueblo.

Wilmsen, Edwin N.
    1970   Lithic analysis and cultural influence: A Paleo-Indian case.
              University of Arizona Anthropological Papers 16. Tucson:
              University of Arizona Press.

CHAPTER 4

ARCHAEOLOGICAL TEST EXCAVATIONS
AT TUBAC STATE PARK, ARIZONA

by

Bruce B. Huckell
and
Lisa W. Huckell

for

Arizona State Parks

The Cultural Resource Management Division
Arizona State Museum
University of Arizona

July 1981

On reaching the old Pueblo of Tubac we found that we
were the only inhabitants. There was not a living
soul to be seen as we approached. The old Plaza was
knee-deep with weeds and grass. All around were adobe
houses, with the roofs fallen in and the walls crumbling
to ruin. Door and windows were all gone, having been
carried away by the Mexicans three years ago.

(Browne 1869:147)

In this place [Tubac] one is forcibly reminded of
traveling among the ancient countries of the east.
With its handful of deserted and ruined mud houses,
one and two stories high, with evidences of an attempt
at some previous day, to arches, pillars, columns, etc.,
one is reminded of a Ninevah or a Babylon. These old
ruins seem now to have no ambition but to crumble away
and become things of the past.

(Conklin 1878:308-9)

Table of Contents

List of Figures

List of Tables

Acknowledgments

Thanks are due several people who contributed to the success of this project. Lynn S. Teague, head of the Cultural Resource Management Section of the Arizona State Museum, was the Principal Investigator on the project. Susan A. Brew served as Project Director.

Peter McCartney, Margaret Glass, and Lee Fratt generously donated their time to assist in the field phase of the testing. The backhoe work carried out by Jim Peachey greatly expedited maximum data recovery from the trenches. Mr. Leland Crawford, former border patrolman and long-time resident of Tubac, cheerfully shared his photographs, maps, and memories which colorfully depicted the rugged lifestyle that characterized the Tubac of 50 years ago. Dr. Elizabeth Brownell, another Tubac resident, graciously took time out from a busy schedule to provide helpful information drawn from her extensive research into the town's history.

Searching for clues to the past land-uses within the study area proved to be a frustrating task; many people helped to reconstruct this, but the efforts of the library staff at the Arizona Historical Society and Susan Harris, curator of photography at the Western Archeological Center, are particularly appreciated. Pierce Chamberlain and Jay Van Orden of the Arizona Historical Society shared their considerable expertise in historic firearms to help with the identification of the musket barrel band from Feature 3.

A large measure of thanks goes to the staff of the Tubac Presidio State Park: Park Manager Bob Sherman, Russ Radom, Wini Chapman, and Luis Martinez. Their enthusiasm, interest, patience, and ready assistance created an ideal environment in which to conduct archaeology. Our thanks to all of you.

Introduction

In February of 1981, Arizona State Parks contracted with the Cultural Resource Management Section of the Arizona State Museum to conduct archaeological test excavations on a parcel of land contained within Tubac Presidio State Historic Park. The testing was designed to evaluate the archaeological resources lying within the western portion of the park as a first step in long-range planning. The area was known to contain remnants of at least two historic structures as well as a surface scatter of native and imported artifacts, all of which suggested that additional material could be present below the existing ground surface. This tangible evidence, in conjunction with the well-known historic signficance of nearby Tubac Presidio, prompted the decision to test the area in order to determine the nature, depth, and extent of subsurface cultural materials so that responsible management policies could be developed for them.

With these objectives in mind, Arizona State Parks approved and authorized the testing program proposed by CRMS. Between May 11 and May 19, 1981, Arizona State Museum archaeologists Bruce B. Huckell and Lisa W. Huckell carried out the testing program with the assistance of three graduate student volunteers from the University of Arizona Department of Anthropology. A total of 22 person-days was devoted to the field phase of the program.

Environmental Setting

Tubac is located in the Santa Cruz River Valley approximately 45 miles (72 km) south of Tucson. It is situated in Township 21S, Range 13E, SE 1/4 of Section 7. The town is located on a low terrace that overlooks the Santa Cruz River which passes by the village immediately to the east. In addition to its strategic military value, the presidio location offered additional inducements to eager would-be settlers: fertile, arable lands, an adequate water supply, ready access to wood for fuel and construction material, both locally and in the nearby Santa Rita Mountains to the northeast, and an abundance of native grasses to sustain herds of livestock.

The area under investigation for the project is part of the existing State Park property, and is located west of the old presidio (AZ DD:8:33) and school house (AZ DD:8:10). The northern boundaries are formed by St. Ann's Church and Church Street to the north, while the western limit is formed by Burruel Street, The southern boundary is somewhat irregular due to private landholdings, but it basically parallels the alley that permits access to the Park's visitors' center (Figure 1).

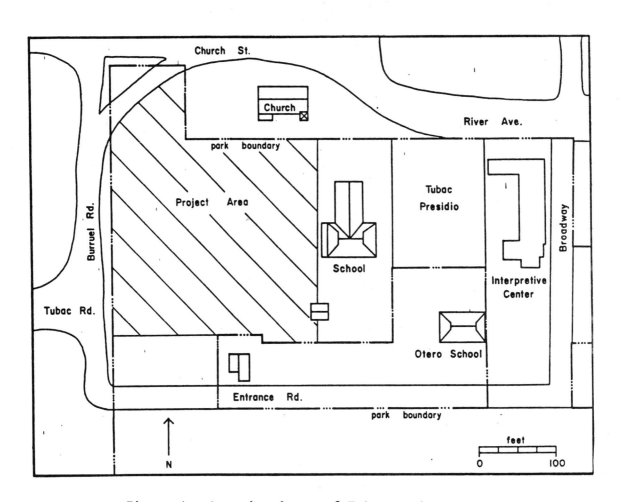

Figure 1.   Locational map of Tubac project area

        The study area has undergone considerable disturbance due to its
close proximity to the church and presidio, which traditionally formed the
nucleus of successive settlement efforts. After the construction of the
schoolhouse in 1885, the study area became the playground for the students.
A large cement slab suitable for playing court games was installed to the
northwest of the school and just south of the church, while the western
portion of the land was made into a baseball diamond. Part of this
process apparently involved attempts to level the somewhat rolling,
irregular ground surface to facilitate ball playing. The school ceased
to function in 1963. From the time the land was acquired by the Arizona
State Parks, it has been mowed regularly several times a year to control
weeds, with large rocks and cobbles that could inhibit the mower's progress
removed from the surface. Today, a dirt access road passes through the
southern portion of the property, and a few large, isolated mesquite trees
are present around the parcel's periphery. The study area had also
recently been partitioned into two parcels by a north-south running wire
and post fence. Figure 2 illustrates a portion of the area that was tested.

Methodology

        The field phase of the project commenced with the archaeologists
carefully walking over the study area several times in order to determine
the extent of known architectural remains and to locate any additional

Figure 2. Photograph of Tubac project area

surface features or artifact concentrations. A primary mapping datum
point was then arbitrarily established in the western section of the
property. The arbitrary division of the land made by the wire fence was
used to divide the parcel into two subunits, with Locus A to the west and
Locus B to the east (Figure 3). A secondary mapping datum was also placed
in Locus B. The datum points were initially used to construct a grid
system for the entire site by means of a transit which guided the placement of excavation units and backhoe trenches. At the conclusion of
the fieldwork, a plane table map was made of the site showing all
boundaries, features, architectural remains, surrounding buildings,
important isolated artifacts, excavation units and trenches.

The need to ascertain as much as possible about the area's research
potential in the most efficient manner resulted in the extensive use of a
backhoe. A series of north-south oriented trenches was established in
both loci; all were tied into the same grid system. A total of 10 trenches
was placed in Locus A, all of which were situated at 5-m intervals
(except for Trench 18). Fewer trenches (seven) were excavated in Locus B,
as they were spaced 10 m apart. The lengths also varied from trench to
trench in order to accommodate surface features, but most were either
25 m or 18 m in length. The depth of the completed trenches seldom
exceeded a meter. During the operation of the backhoe, a monitor observed
the progress and checked for any cultural materials brought up by the
bucket. The finished trenches were closely examined for artifacts or
features and were then profiled if features were present.

Because the remnants of two structures had been found within the
study area, special attention was devoted to attempting to identify their
age, function, cultural affiliation, history, etc., through existing
records encountered during the research phase of the project. Several
information sources were investigated. The excellent studies by Bents
(1949) and Dobyns (1959) provided an invaluable general historical
framework as well as some helpful, more specific data. The Arizona State
Museum site survey and additional site information files were consulted
as was ASM's photograph collection. The University of Arizona Library,
Special Collections Division, was also checked for information concerning
the project area, as was the map collection in the main library. Several
of the Arizona Historical Society collections were reviewed, including
photographs, maps, interview transcripts, manuscripts, and books. The
photograph files at the Western Archeological Center were also checked.
Government Land Office maps on file at the State Historic Preservation
Office in Phoenix were also examined for us by Frank Fryman. Additional
information was provided by Tubac residents Dr. Elizabeth Brownell and
Mr. Leland Crawford. Unfortunately, lack of time and the limited scope
of work required for the project precluded the investigation of all
potential information leads.

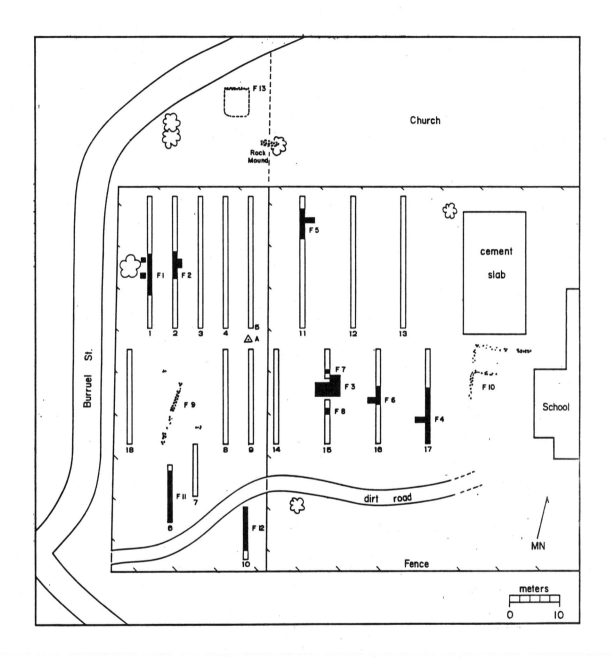

Figure 3. Map of test excavations in the Tubac project area (1-18 = trench numbers, F = features)

Features

Feature 1

A thin ash lens and underlying trash deposit exposed in the east and west walls of Trench 1 was designated Feature 1 (Figure 3). Averaging 4 cm in thickness, this ash lens consisted of light gray to dark gray powdery ash that extended for a distance of 7.8 m on a north-south axis. It lay between 3 cm and 10 cm below the present ground surface and undulated slightly in elevation. Mixed historic and recent trash occurred above the ash lens, and some bone and a very few artifacts were encountered below it. This lower deposit was a graded, laminated reddish brown sand that gave way to a massive reddish brown sand with dispersed pebbles and cobbles. Two 1 m-by-1 m test squares were excavated into this feature on the west side of Trench 1; both yielded little in terms of artifacts. The test squares also indicated that the ash lens did not continue too far to the west of the trench; in one square it pinched out 25 cm west of the trench and in the other it disappeared between 50 cm and 60 cm west of the trench.

Feature 2

Trench 2 cut through a shallow, bowl-shaped pit that was designated Feature 2 (Figure 3). Measuring approximately 5 m on a north-south axis and displaying a maximum depth of 50 cm below present ground surface, this feature appears to have served as a trash pit. A relatively large quantity of artifacts was recovered from the area of the feature during the backhoe trenching, and the pair of 1 m-by-1 m test squares placed on the east side of the trench also yielded a number of artifacts. The fill of the pit generally consisted of grayish brown silty, gravelly sand with dispersed artifacts and cobbles. This fill was intruded into a coarse reddish brown sand with abundant dispersed artifacts and cobbles. This fill was intruded into a coarse reddish brown sand with abundant dispersed pebbles, which was in turn underlain by a calcified cobble to small boulder gravel. Figure 4 shows a cross section through this feature.

Feature 3

Prior to the cutting of Trench 15 in Locus B, a relatively dense concentration of potsherds was observed on the surface just slightly to the north of the midpoint of the trench (Figure 3). It was designated Feature 3, and a decision was made to test it by hand excavation rather than with the backhoe. Two 2 m-by-2 m test squares were first constructed on an east-west alignment, perpendicular to the path of the proposed trench; a third square was later added to the northeast. The trench (15) was then split into two portions, both of which terminated within 50 cm to 75 cm of the test squares. The hand excavations and the backhoe trenches

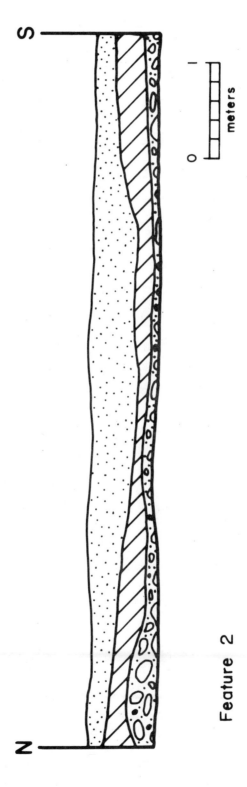

Feature 2

Figure 4. Profile of Feature 2

indicated that the feature extended for approximately 5 m on a north-south axis, but seldom exceeded 5 cm to 10 cm in thickness. The surface artifact distribution suggested a similar east-west length. Two deep cylindrical pit features, designated Features 7 and 8, were encountered in the northern and southern halves of Trench 15 respectively; their relationships to Feature 3, if any, are not clear.

Feature 3 consisted of concentrated artifacts in a matrix of grayish brown silty, gravelly, sand that lay unconformably on a reddish brown silty sand. This features produced the greatest number, density, and diversity of artifacts of the features investigated during the project. The high concentration of artifacts, coupled with the shallowness of the deposit, implied a trash deposit that had accumulated through time in a shallow declivity of probable natural origin.

Feature 4

An ash lens and trash deposit similar in form to Feature 1 was encountered in Trench 17, and was labeled Feature 4 (Figure 3). Measuring nearly 12 m on a north-south axis and ranging from 25 cm to 60 cm below the present ground surface, this feature was tested with a 1 m-wide by 2.5 m-long test trench. The test trench revealed four strata: 1) a light grayish brown gravelly sand up to 25 cm in thickness overlying 2) a 2-cm to 4-cm thick lens of loose, fine, light gray ash superposed above 3) a poorly consolidated grayish brown gravelly sand with numerous dispersed cobbles which rested upon 4) a coarse cobble gravel (Figure 5). Stratum 1 yielded mixed historic trash, while Stratum 2, the ash lens, contained numerous tiny cinders and slivers of heavily burned bone. Stratum 3 produced several unburned animal bones but few artifacts. This feature, or at least this portion of the feature, seems to have served initially as a place where waste from slaughtering and butchering was deposited, and later became a dump for the ashes cleaned out of fireplaces or stoves. Mixed trash was then deposited above the ash lens.

Feature 5

At the north end of Trench 11, a shallow pit was encountered (Figure 3): it was designated Feature 5. Visible in both walls of the trench, it presented the appearance of a bowl-shaped depression measuring approximately 6 m on a north-south axis and achieving a maximum depth of 70 cm below present ground surface. The fill of the pit was grayish brown in color, and was composed of a silty sand with dispersed pebbles, charcoal flecks, and artifacts. The feature is overlain by 10 cm to 25 cm of loose reddish brown sand, and has been intruded into a consolidated reddish brown gravelly sand. A short cross trench was cut perpendicular to Trench 11 through the center of the pit to further evaluate its size and contents. This trench revealed that the feature extended approximately 2 m to the east, but that it contained very few artifacts.

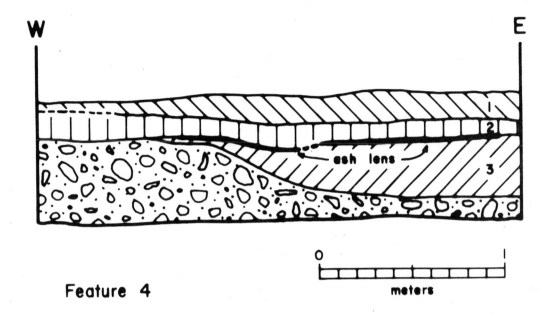

W   E

ash lens

1
2
3

Feature 4

0   1

meters

Figure 5. Profile of test excavation unit at Feature 4

Feature 6

Near the center of Trench 16 another pit was located (Figure 3).
Labeled Feature 6, this feature was somewhat deeper relative to its
length than Features 2 and 5, and exhibited steeper side walls. It
measured approximately 2.5 m on a north-south axis and slightly less than
50 cm in maximum thickness. It was filled with a light grayish brown
silty sand with occasional pebbles, charcoal flecks, and a few artifacts. A 1 m-by-1 m test square was placed on the western side of the
trench toward the southern third of the exposed feature. Its excavation
revealed that the feature continued only approximately 85 cm to the west;
its bottom was marked by a distinct change to a compacted reddish brown
gravelly sand. A few artifacts and bone fragments were recovered from
the pit. Most of these came from the pit's upper half.

Feature 7

A small pit which presented a nearly square cross section was observed in the east wall of the north half of Trench 15 (Figure 3). Designated Feature 7, it measured approximately 90 cm in width by 80 cm in depth and was filled with a well-compacted, light grayish brown silty, gravelly sand. It was in turn overlain by the trash deposit of Feature 3 and thus probably predates that feature. It received no hand test excavation.

Feature 8

In the south half of Trench 15 approximately 8 m south of Feature 7 another pit nearly square in cross section was exposed (Figure 3). Feature 8, as it was designated, was observed on both trench walls and measured approximately 70 cm to 80 cm in width by 70 cm in depth. Three separate fill events were visible in the pit. Stratum 3 was a 5-cm to 10-cm thick layer of grayish brown, ashy silt at the bottom of the pit, and was overlain by Stratum 2, a 10-cm thick unit of apparently sterile, reddish brown gravelly coarse sand. The remainder of the pit contained a mottled grayish brown silty sand with occasional inclusions of reddish brown clayey, silty sand designated Stratum 1. The lack of time precluded any hand testing of this feature.

Feature 9

Visible on the surface in the southwestern quarter of Locus A on a slight rise was a linear arrangement of cobbles aligned on a magnetic north-south axis (Figure 3). This cobble alignment measured approximately 12.5 m in length, and maintained a fairly constant width of between 75 cm and 80 cm, although after the alignment had been cleared of dirt and vegetation it was found that there were gaps or discontinuities in it. No east-west trending alignments that intersected the main north-south alignment were located, although one possible segment of such an alignment was identified 4.9 m to the east, and a small cluster of five larger cobbles occurred 3.2 m west of the north end of the main alignment (Figure 3). The cobbles composing the alignment ranged from 10 cm to 30 cm in maximum dimension, and all were of locally available materials.

Figure 6a shows the alignment after initial exposure. Figure 6b shows a wall footing of the Fish House in Tucson and its relationship to the above-ground wall. This cobble alignment is clearly the remains of a footing or foundation for an adobe wall. Such footings are not infrequently constructed this way, "...bringing the rock foundations above exterior grade to avoid groundwater and rain" (McHenry 1973:42), and may be seen on many surviving adobe structures. In the case of Feature 9, the remnants of this footing are a single cobble in thickness and were found to be resting on a culturally sterile hard reddish brown sandy

Figure 6. a) Photograph of Feature 9 cobble alignments;
b) wall footing at Fish House in Tucson and
its relationship to the above-ground wall

gravel. No residue from adobe bricks was identifiable, nor was the
terrain around the footing at all mounded. This suggests that the
structure or wall which once stood on this location was razed to ground
level or perhaps slightly deeper in some areas. Extremely few artifacts
were present on the surface around Feature 9, and Trench 18 excavated to
the west of Feature 9 (Figure 3) revealed no cultural deposits or
artifacts.

Feature 10

At the far eastern end of Locus B, immediatly west of the former
school building, were a series of three intersecting cobble alignments
which together formed a single "F"-shaped figure (Figure 3). Designated
Feature 10, these alignments are footings for some sort of building, but
an unknown portion of the footings has been removed at the southern and
eastern edges of the feature. Like Feature 9, the footings are composed
of a single layer of locally available cobbles measuring 10 cm to 30 cm
in maximum dimension. The northernmost east-west aligned footing measures
approximately 11.2 m in length, and displays an average width of 64 cm.
The easternmost part of this footing may have been an independent segment

3.0 m in length; it bears definite ends that appear to have been intentionally constructed as such. In addition, this segment rests in what appears to be a shallow trench cut into the native red clayey sandy gravel. The cobbles were set into this trench which was then filled with a chocolate-colored, organic, clayey silt. Other parts of the Feature 10 footings do not display this sort of construction, and elsewhere the cobbles simply rest directly upon the reddish brown native sediments. In short, it seems that this segment may have been constructed independently from the remainder of the alignment to accommodate one or two doorways on the north wall of the structure. One of these doorways would have been to the west of the segment and one to the east; unfortunately no more of the footings are preserved to the east of the segment to document the existence of the second door.

The second east-west aligned footing and the north-south oriented footing are both incomplete, probably having been destroyed during the building of the school in 1885 or during additions to it made in the 1920s or 1930s. In present form the second east-west footing measures approximately 4.4 m in length by approximately 65 cm in width, while the north-south footing displays a length of approximately 10 m by 65 cm in width. Again no trace of adobe bricks or brick residue was present around Feature 10, suggesting that it was completely razed. Probably during the course of this demolition, the southern and eastern footings, as well as the southern end of the western footing, were completely removed.

Feature 11

The southern third of Trench 6 revealed part of another shallow pit and an associated layer of sheet trash extending northward nearly to the northern end of the trench (Figure 3). As exposed, the pit measured approximately 3.1 m on a north-south axis; assuming that the feature had a rough symmetry in its cross section, this represents half or slightly less of the total length of Feature 11. It achieves a maximum depth of 50 cm. Filling this pit and also extending northward from it as a thin layer for approximately 4.4 m is a gray silty sand filled with dispersed pebbles and artifacts (Figure 7). At the base of the pit is a 2.3 cm-thick layer of dark gray ashy earth. Both the pit and the layer rest unconformably on reddish brown silty, gravelly sand with numerous pebbles and cobbles. Due to the time limitations, this feature was not test excavated, although a small sample of artifacts was obtained from the walls of the trench and the backhoe backdirt. Its proximity to Feature 9, the footing for a possible structure, suggests that this feature may be associated with it.

Feature 12

Exposed over all but the southernmost 2 meters of Trench 10 was a trash deposit labeled Feature 12 (Figure 3). The abundant trash occurred as a nearly continuous level for a north-south distance of

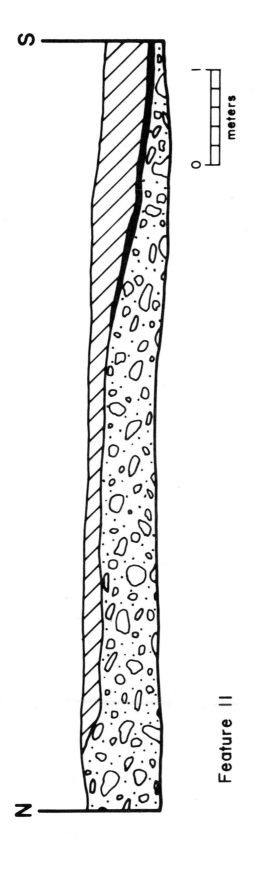

Feature 11

meters

Figure 7.   Profile of Feature 11

8.0 m, and yielded numerous objects of early 20th century age as well as a few older items. This level lay approximately 45 cm to 50 cm below the present ground surface, and was contained in a unit of brown silty sand. It was not tested by hand, but a sample of the artifacts it contained was gathered from the walls of the trench and the backhoe spoil dirt.

Feature 13

At the extreme northern end of Locus A there is a small piece of State Parks property that extends all the way to Church Street (Figure 1). Measuring approximately 23.25 m north-south by 35.00 m east-west, this parcel contains Feature 13, a low mound and a single east-west running cobble alignment (Figure 3). The cobble alignment is interpreted as a wall footing. It measures 5.2 m in length by 45 cm to 50 cm in width, and lies at the northern edge of the low mound. No other footings joining this one were located, but it is entirely possible that these lie under the low mound. The mound itself contains scattered pieces of cement, wire, and wood, and seems to represent the remains of a small building. Immediately to the east of the mound was a crushed door knob and door lock mechanism, further suggesting the former presence of a structure in this locality. The surface of the area around the mound contains relatively abundant historic trash representing both the 19th and 20th centuries. No backhoe trenching was done in this area, due to the obvious presence of archaeological remains. A small series of hand excavations was made to follow out the wall footing and to investigate certain features of the mound, and the area was mapped with a plane table and alidade.

Four meters southeast of the southeastern corner of the mound was an elongated pile of cobbles measuring 3.5 m long by 1.4 m wide by nearly 1 m in height. The significance of this cobble pile and its relationship to Feature 13 or the church just to the east is not clear.

Discussion

The features defined in the two loci during the testing indicate that these areas formerly contained domestic structures and the sorts of related features commonly associated with them; in short, this was part and parcel of the village of Tubac. It seems probable that the three cobble alignment wall footings, Features 9, 10, and 13, represent the locations of former buildings. Seven of the other features appear to be trash-filled depressions or pits, while the remaining two features seem to be deeper square or cylindrical pits without trash in their fills.

The combination of later disturbance and a lack of documentation severely limit what can be said about the cobble wall footings described above. The buildings were razed, and even the footings themselves were partially removed; therefore it is not possible to discuss the sizes, plans, or construction of these features. In the case of Feature 9 in

Locus A, only a single alignment remained of what may have been the footings for a building. The second difficulty is that none of the known historic documents aid in the identification or reconstruction of these structures. Examination of the known maps, photographs, and manuscripts reveals that only one map, that of Urrutia in 1766 (Shenk and Teague 1975: Figure 2), is of any aid. It shows only that at that time a single structure was present just slightly to the south of the church. If the present church is in the same location as the first church, it is possible that Feature 9 is all that remains of the small structure. However, given the sketch-map nature of Urrutia's plan, it is impossible to establish such an identification with any certainty.

One additional map was discovered that ostensibly portrays the presidio of Tubac (North 1980:83). However, the representation is radically different from that given by Urrutia, eyewitnesses (Hinton 1954:187; Shenk and Teague 1975: Figure 3), and the archaeological record (Shenk and Teague 1975). The presidio is shown as a very large, completely enclosed, somewhat compressed octagon which contains several isolated buildings. A copy of the map in the possession of Leland Crawford is dated 1858. This fact, in conjunction with the labels presented in English and the notation "suitable for a store" under one of the interior buildings, suggests that the map may have been used for promotional purposes, perhaps by Charles Poston and Herman Ehrenberg as they solicited financial support in the east for mining ventures in the Tubac vicinity. However, the scale, features, placement and conformation of the presidio strongly suggest that the map was drawn by someone who had never been to Tubac. Its value must be considered questionable at present.

It has been amply documented (Bents 1949) that the history of Tubac is one of repeated episodes of settlement, abandonment forced by Apache raiding pressure, and resettlement. The two quotations presented at the beginning of the report reflect the condition in which Tubac was found by visitors shortly after its last major abandonment: the quotations also show how quickly the buildings in the village became ruined. Although some of the houses and other buildings saw repeated use during reoccupations of the presidio area, many undoubtedly steadily deteriorated and disappeared. Bents (1949:189) found some indications that as part of an episode of renewed community growth in the late 1870s, some of the old ruined buildings were gradually razed and replaced with new adobe houses. A proposed "Plan for the Tubac Townsite" was drawn up in 1878 to act as a guideline for anticipated growth. Several existing buildings are shown on the map, including the presidio and church ruins, with most of the actively used properties being present in the area south and east of the presidio. No structures are indicated within what would be the two loci considered in this report.

Because the school was constructed in 1885, it is clear that the destruction of Feature 10 must predate the construction of that building, and, by extension, it can be argued that Feature 9 also predates the school. Unfortunately, none of the existing maps or photographs offer any clues as to the identity of Feature 10. Feature 13, positioned outside school property to the northwest, does not necessarily predate 1885; its history is not so clearly linked to the building of the school. Although it cannot be dated or identified with a particular function at this time, it is actually in the best state of preservation of the three features. It may therefore be viewed as retaining some research potential, an attribute not shared by either Feature 9 or 10.

The other features identified in the tested area are also some-what difficult to interpret. Certainly most of these are trash-filled or contain some artifacts, but their origins are less clear. It is possible that some of these features represent intentionally excavated pits. These may have been dug as trash or garbage pits or even as material (adobe) borrow pits; examples of these are Features 1, 2, 4, 5, 6, 11, and 12. Two of the other pits, Features 7 and 8, are of uncertain shape and function, and do not seem to be trash-filled. Finally, Feature 3 is interpreted as a trash accumulation emplaced in a shallow depression of probable natural origin.

As noted in the discussion of the artifacts obtained from them, the nature of these features appears to be directly related to domestic functions. The artifacts are almost all household objects or refuse such as bone and ash from houses. While it is not possible to specifi-cally date all of the individual pit features, all but Feature 12 contain artifacts that appear to be of 19th century origin. Probable dates may be given for three features. Despite some admixture of more recent arti-facts, it is suggested that Features 2, 3, and 4 represent the Middle Period (1800 to 1850) as defined by Shenk and Teague (1975). There-fore, these features date to the Mexican occupation of Tubac. Features 1, 5, 6, and 11 may also date to this period, though insufficient samples of datable artifacts prevent their definite inclusion in this occupation. No artifacts were recovered from Feature 7 and 8, so their ages cannot be inferred except by their stratigraphic positions. Finally, Feature 12 appears to date to the first half of the 20th century. With the exception of the latter feature, all of the other pits retain research potential, some more than others. Those which seem to be most valuable in this regard are Features 2, 3, 4, and 11.

Material Culture

The backhoe trenching and limited hand test excavations produced a small sample of artifacts from a variety of features. These artifacts provide information concerning the relative areas of particular features and their functions. They may also aid in the identification of the ethnic character of the residents and the construction of their socio-economic patterns. For the purposes of this report and for establishing the relative importance of the remains which were located, the chronological and functional implications of the artifacts will be emphasized. Individual portions of the artifact assemblage will be presented separately. Each aspect of the assemblage will be described briefly, and its distribution through the features will be summarized in table format. For the sake of comparison, the tripartite division of the occupation of Tubac utilized by Shenk and Teague (1975) will be followed here; that is, the Early Period (1750-1800), Middle Period (1800-1850), and Late Period (1850-1900).

Indigenous Artifacts

Ceramics

Broken pieces of pottery produced by the indigenous population of Pima Indians were the most abundant artifact type recovered during the testing. Analysis of the potsherds was done by separating them into the following types: Papago Plain, an undecorated brown utility ware; Papago Red, characterized by the application of a red clay slip to the interior, exterior, or both surfaces of the vessel; Papago Red-on-brown, basically Papago Plain with the addition of a red painted design; and Papago Glaze, another decorated type with designs done in matte red paint and green lead glaze paint. In addition, sherds of all types that retained portions of the vessel rim were classified as to whether they represented jars or bowls. Sherds which were smaller in size than a nickel were classified as "too small" and were separated into plain and red categories. Table 1 presents the occurrence of the potsherds in the features described in the preceding section.

As is commonly the case, Papago Plain is the most abundant type, accounting for 80 percent of the total ceramic assemblage. While some variation was observed in the surface finish and temper characteristics, this type appears to be quite consistent with that described by Fontana and others (1962) as well as by Shenk and Teague (1975) and Robinson (1976) for sites in southern Arizona. Jars are somewhat more abundant than bowls in this sample, as was true for the collection obtained from the Tubac Presidio excavations (Shenk and Teague 1975:60). Four rim sherds, all representing jars, showed the presence of a separate rim coil; the remainder of the rims displayed only a slightly thickened lip. The use of the rim coil is regarded as a 19th century treatment, probably disappearing by the turn of the century. Just how much before that the thickened-lip treatment was adopted is unknown, but appears to have started before 1850.

The sherds classified as Papago Red (19.2 percent of the assemblage) are also good matches for previously described samples of this type. Bowls outnumber jars by a factor of more than 2:1 in the small sample obtained from the testing; this is again consistent with the findings of Shenk and Teague (1975:61).

Only five decorated sherds, all quite small, were recovered from the testing, and all came from Feature 3. These account for slightly

Table 1.   Indigenous ceramics from the Tubac testing project

	Papago Plain		Papago Red		Papago Red-on-Brown		Papago Glaze		Too Small		
	Rims	Body	Rims	Body	Rims	Body	Rims	Body	Plain	Red	Total
Feature 1	-	3	-	-	-	-	-	-	2	1	6
Feature 2	1/1*	16	-	3	-	-	-	-	13	-	34
Feature 3	18/7	147	4/7	43	-	4	-	1	232	55	518
Feature 4	0/1	18	0/1	1	-	-	-	-	20	3	44
Feature 5	0/3	6	-	-	-	-	-	-	1	-	10
Trench 1	-	3	0/1	-	-	-	-	-	1	-	5
Trench 2	-	2	-	-	-	-	-	-	-	-	2
Trench 6	-	6	-	1	-	-	-	-	3	1	11
Trench 8	0/1	3	0/1	-	-	-	-	-	-	1	6
Trench 10	-	-	-	-	-	-	-	-	1	-	1
Trench 17	-	8	-	1	-	-	-	-	1	-	10
Total	19/13	212	4/10	49	-	4	-	1	274	61	647

*Note: Jars/Bowls

less than 0.8 percent of the total assemblage, a figure fairly consistent
with the observations of Shenk and Teague (1975:62-4). Of interest is
the presence of the single Papago Glaze sherd in the collection and the
absence of any Papago Black-on-red. The former type tends to be slightly
earlier in time, dating from the 18th to the mid-19th centuries (Fontana
and others 1962:103-09) while the latter type began to be produced
sometime during the mid-19th century.

Ceramics produced by the Pima undoubtedly served as the
standard tableware and cooking vessels for the people of Tubac. The pottery was well constructed, probably inexpensive, and readily available,
as witnessed by remarks printed in The Arizonian in 1859. In speaking of
the local Indian population it was remarked that

> They [the Papagos] have been of some utility here, in performing
> manual labor, making and selling hay for horses, and in supply-
> ing the town, especially the Mexican population with earthen
> wares for kitchen use (The Arizonian as quoted in Bents 1949:
> 136).

Given local production by groups of semipermanent Pima residents of
Tubac, the abundance of this class of artifacts is not surprising.

Flaked Stone

Thirty-five pieces of flaked stone were recovered during the
testing phase work. Of this number, 31 were unmodified, unutilized
pieces of waste (debitage) from the manufacture of stone tools. Table 2
summarizes the proveniences and material types of these specimens.

Four finished flaked stone artifacts were identified. One of
these is a projectile point from Feature 4 missing a small portion of its
tip (Figure 8). Made of basalt, it displays a shape and manufacture
technique identical to that of historic Papago projectile points (Haury
1950:274, Figure 56 j-2). Feature 3 yielded a unifacially retouched
scraper made of rhyolitic jasper and one small piece of chalcedony
(burned) with a partially bifacial retouch. The latter specimen was too
incomplete to assign to any formal tool type. The final specimen is a
large, crude, bifacially flaked implement recovered from Trench 15 in
Locus B.

The presence of these flaked stone artifacts may be explained by
the addition of prehistoric specimens to historic contexts, or by continued manufacture and use of flaked stone tools by the Pimans in
historic times. It is probable that both situations are operative at
Tubac.

Two other artifacts of flaked stone that may be of native manufacture should also be mentioned at this time. Both are gunflints, one
of which is apparently manufactured of locally available chalcedony;

Table 2. Flaked stone debitage from the Tubac testing project

	Rhyolitic Jasper	Basalt	Rhyolite	Quartzite	Chert	Chalcedony	Total
Feature 1	1	-	-	-	1	1	3
Feature 2	2	-	-	-	3	-	5
Feature 3	4	3	1	1	4	3	16
Feature 4	5	-	-	-	1	-	6
Trench 2	-	-	1	-	-	-	1
Total	12	3	2	1	9	4	31

the other may or may not have been locally made. Figure 8 illustrates both. The specimen that is certainly of local manufacture (Figure 8) shows little wear, while the other, of gray chert or flint, has been relatively heavily used (Figure 8). Feature 3 produced the chalcedony gunflint, but the chert specimen was a surface find in the southwestern part of Locus B. Shenk and Teague (1975) reported both locally made and imported gunflints from the presidio area excavations.

Ground Stone

Feature 3 yielded the only ground stone artifact recovered from the testing. This was a mano of dark gray vesicular basalt made from a sub-square cobble. Measuring 10.5 cm by 11.5 cm in plan and 8 cm in thickness, this mano showed signs of wear on both surfaces. The specimen could be either of prehistoric or historic age; it is known that both the Pima and the Spanish/Mexican settlers utilized the mano and metate for the grinding of seeds into flour.

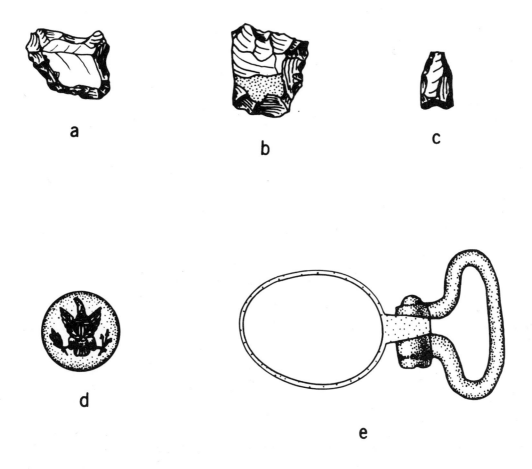

Figure 8. Tubac testing project artifacts:
a) gunflint; b) gunflint; c) projectile point;
d) U.S. Army coat button; e) musket barrel
band and sling swivel

Table 3.   Nonindigenous ceramics from the Tubac testing project

| | White Earthenware | Majolica | | Green Glaze | Porcelain | Total |
		White	Decorated			
Feature 1	-	-	-	1	-	1
Feature 2	2	1	1	5	-	9
Feature 3	4	3	2	3	3	15
Feature 4	-	-	1	-	-	1
Trench 2	-	-	-	1	-	1
Trench 8	-	-	-	1	-	1
Trench 15	7	-	-	-	-	7
Total	13	4	4	11	3	35

Nonindigenous Artifacts

The remainder of the artifacts found during the testing are the products of European technology, though not necessarily of European manufacture. These artifacts may be divided into four groups: ceramics, metal objects, glass, and a miscellaneous grouping of various objects and materials. Each of these is briefly described in the following sections.

Ceramics

Four general categories of nonindigenous ceramics were recognized in the small sample of sherds (35) from the testing. Table 3 presents these categories and their distribution. The first of these is simply a white earthenware, principally English in origin, with a vitreous white glaze and cream to white paste. Thirteen sherds of this ware, all small and undecorated, were recovered from the testing operations (Table 3). These cannot be dated with any precision, except to say that the specimens probably postdate 1820.

Eight sherds of Mexican majolica were found in association with features or in trenches, and another three sherds were collected from the surface. Majolica, or "maiolica" as it is sometimes spelled, had its origins in Spain, but factories for its production in Mexico were established shortly after the conquest in the mid-16th century (Lister and Lister 1975). Mass-produced and relatively inexpensive, majolica was shipped and marketed throughout New Spain, and continues to be produced today (Lister and Lister 1972). Produced in a long-lived series of different plain and decorated types, it has been found at Spanish and Mexican period sites in Arizona such as Quiburi (Di Peso 1953), Tubac (Shenk and Teague 1975), and Guevavi (Robinson 1976). Barnes (1972) has summarized the kinds of majolica known from southern Arizona sites and their relative dates of manufacture.

The sample from the testing project includes four plain white sherds, four sherds identifiable only as one of the blue-on-white decorated types, one sherd of polychrome majolica with green and dark brown decoration, and three sherds of San Elizario Polychrome, a blue-on-white type with added black-to-brown framing lines (Gerald 1968:45-52). San Elizario Polychrome apparently dates from approximately 1750 to perhaps as late as 1850 (Shenk and Teague 1975; Barnes 1972). One of the San Elizario Polychrome sherds was associated with Feature 3, one came from Trench 10, and one was from the surface of Locus B.

Eleven sherds of a red paste earthenware bearing a green slip were found (Table 3). Generally, these are classified generically as "olive jar" green glaze types; the sample from the testing shows considerable variation. Two sherds bear a light green to olive drab glaze on the interior surface only, three show a darker green glaze on both the interior and exterior surfaces, and six have an emerald green glaze on both surfaces. The former two varieties appear to be typical of "olive jars" (Caywood 1950:86), but the latter half dozen specimens may be of a type called Guanajuato Green Glaze (Caywood 1950:85-6). Dating of these types is poor, but Shenk and Teague (1975:94-5) note their greatest abundance in Early and Middle Period contexts (1750-1850).

Finally, three tiny sherds of finely made porcelain were recovered from Feature 3. Two are undecorated and the third bears only a blue painted band around the rim. These sherds appear to be typical of Chinese porcelain which was imported into Mexico in large quantities from approximately 1600 onwards through the Colonial Period (Caywood 1950:83-5; Shenk and Teague 1975:92-4). Caywood (1950:84) suggests that it too was widespread on the northern frontier, probably being transported into the Pimería Alta along with majolica and green glaze wares.

Metal

A surprisingly small quantity of metal artifacts was recovered from the testing, but this small sample included a number of diverse forms. Table 4 lists the forms and proveniences of those metal objects

Table 4. Metal artifacts from the Tubac testing project

	Can Fragments	Square Nails	Wire Nails	Fence Staples	Rivets (Iron)	Tacks (Iron)	Screws/Bolts	Wire	Horseshoes	Pencil Eraser Sleeves	Bottle Cap	Screw-on Cap	Unknown Iron	Unknown Brass	Unknown Lead	Total
Feature 2	-	4[a]	-	-	-	-	-	-	-	-	-	-	2	-	-	6
Feature 3	4	4[b]	-	1	1	2	1	5	-	1	1	-	1	1	2	24
Feature 4	-	1	-	-	-	2	-	-	-	1	-	-	1	-	-	5
Feature 6	-	-	-	-	-	-	-	1	-	-	-	-	-	-	-	1
Trench 2	-	-	-	-	-	-	-	-	1	-	-	-	-	-	-	1
Trench 6	-	-	-	-	-	-	-	-	-	-	-	-	1	-	-	1
Trench 8	1	-	-	-	-	-	-	-	-	-	-	-	-	-	-	1
Trench 10	7	-	1	-	-	-	1	2	-	-	-	1	-	-	-	12
Total	12	9	1	1	1	4	2	8	1	2	1	1	5	1	2	51

[a] Includes 3 horsehoe nails

[b] Two hand wrought

that have little value as temporal indicators; a few of the more interesting or temporally useful artifacts are described in the following paragraphs.

Feature 3 yielded a brass musket barrel band with an iron sling swivel still attached (Figure 8). Careful comparison of this specimen with specimens in the collections of the Arizona Historical Society and the Arizona State Museum, as well as with photographs of specimens from various museums around the world, has led to a probable identification of the musket from which this specimen originated. It seems most likely that this is the middle barrel band from a snaphaunce (flintlock) infantry musket manufactured in Spain during the first decade of the 19th century; those specimens of this model which were examined or described bore manufacture dates ranging between 1802 and 1807 on their barrels. One of these muskets is described and illustrated by Brinckerhoff and Chamberlain (1972:36-7, Plates 33-35), who refer to it as the Model 1803. The presence of the barrel band may suggest repairs to a musket that had been damaged in service to the extent that this particular band was no longer useful.

Feature 3 also yielded part of another iron sling swivel, a gun flint, and a deformed lead musket ball. Unfortunately the second sling swivel fragment is too incomplete to attribute to any particular model of musket. The ball, deformed though it is, may originally have been of a sufficiently large caliber to have been fired in the musket represented by the barrel band (approximately 18.6 mm or .73 inch caliber).

Feature 6 also yielded firearms-related metal artifacts in the form of two musket percussion caps. One has been fired and is broken and deformed; the other is apparently unfired and is complete. Percussion weapons were popular and widespread between 1830 and the Civil War, and were rendered obsolete by the development of metallic cartridge firing weapons during the 1860's and 1870's.

From just above the ash lens in Feature 4, a Liberty Seated type U.S. dime was found. Dated 1864 and minted at San Francisco, the coin is in very fine condition and apparently saw little circulation prior to its loss at Tubac.

The backdirt from the backhoe excavation of Trench 1 yielded a single U.S. Army coat button (Figure 8). This particular style is known as the General Service button, and was in use between 1855 and 1884. The backing of the button bears the stamp of the Waterbury Button Company. American troops were stationed at Tubac periodically during the 1850's and 1860's.

Three lead discs of different diameters were recovered from Feature 3. One is 3/8 inch (10 mm) in diameter, one is 1/2 inch (12 mm) and the third is 7/8 inch (20 mm); all vary between 1 mm and 3 mm in thickness. None bore any markings, and their function is not known.

The metal artifacts listed in Table 4 aid little in establishing dates for the features or trenches in which they were found. Some, such as the bottle cap, pencil eraser sleeve, modern machine screw, wire, and fence staple found in Feature 3, are most likely more recent artifacts intrusive into older contexts. Others, such as the square nails from that same feature, may or may not be intrusive, but have long histories with few changes. Their value as dating devices is thus minimal and they add little to an understanding of the feature from which they came.

Glass

Despite the fact that 162 pieces of glass and one glass bead were recovered from the testing operations, the highly fragmented condition of most of these pieces allows little interpretation of their significance. Table 5 presents a breakdown of the glass by color or type and provenience.

Glass color can be related to age or function in a general way (see Shenk and Teague 1975:104-10), but bottle bases, finishes, large fragments with seams or embossing, or complete specimens are far more useful for these purposes. Only one fragment of a wine bottle finish was found (Feature 3), and only three basal fragments complete enough to be of use were found. The three bases all came from Feature 12, the relatively late trash deposit in Trench 10, and two are clearly 20th century specimens. The third is a very patinated beer bottle base bearing a W.F. & S (probably William Franzen and Son) stamp. It may date to the period between 1900 and 1929 (Toulouse 1971:536-8), and is in all likelihood an older specimen intrusive in this younger trash accumulation.

Seven pieces of household glass (Shenk and Teague 1975:110-11) were found. Four were fragments of a light yellowish green thick-walled vessel, one was a clear glass foot from a candy dish, and two pieces of a clear glass kerosene lamp base were identified. All were found in the Trench 10 backdirt or in place in Feature 12, and so are relatively young.

A single faceted bead of dark blue glass was found on the surface in the southwestern part of Locus A. Measuring 5 mm in length by 5 mm in width, this specimen is of a type quite commonly found in 19th century historic sites throughout the West. Relatively little can be said of its exact period of manufacture.

Finally, two pieces of window glass were identified.

Miscellaneous

This last category of nonindigenous artifacts is basically a catch-all that contains byproducts such as slag and cinders, building materials such as concrete and adobe brick fragments, and classes of

Table 5. Glass from the Tubac testing project

	Bottle or Container									Household		Window Glass	Total
	Black	Green	Brown	Clear	Light Green	Aqua	Purple	Milk	Cobalt	Yellow-Green	Clear		
Feature 1	-	-	1	1	-	-	-	-	-	-	-	1	3
Feature 2	3	4	-	3	1	-	-	-	-	-	-	-	11
Feature 3	1	14	13	14	1	7	1	-	-	-	-	1	52
Feature 4	-	4	1	5	-	5	-	1	-	-	-	-	16
Feature 5	-	-	1	-	-	1	-	-	-	-	-	-	2
Feature 6	-	-	1	1	-	-	-	-	-	-	-	-	2
Trench 2	-	4	1	-	-	-	-	-	-	-	-	-	5
Trench 6	-	-	-	3	1	1	-	-	-	-	-	-	5
Trench 10	-	-	3	45	-	6	4	-	1	4	3	-	64
Total	4	26	21	72	3	20	5	1	1	4	3	2	162

artifacts poorly represented, in this case rubber and electrical items. Table 6 presents the distribution of these artifacts.

Small lumps of glassy slag are distributed throughout the area tested; Shenk and Teague (1975:146) noted a similar situation in the presidio area. They interpreted the slag as the byproduct of coal fuel used in smelting operations, and suggested that the smelting occurred in the vicinity of the presidio. As Table 6 indicates, Feature 4 yielded a relatively large quantity of slag as well as numerous white cinders. The slag was largely present in Stratum 1 of that feature, above the ash lens, while the cinders came from within the ash lens. The cinders and ash may be interpreted as stove or fireplace cleanings, but the origin of the slag is not so clear. While it is certainly possible that small smelters operated within the village of Tubac, it may also be that the slag is the product of blacksmith forges or even coal-fired household stoves.

Construction materials are represented by eight fragments of what appear to be burned adobe bricks and three pieces of concrete. All were found as small fragments in contexts other than architectural features, except for a number of pieces associated with Feature 13 which were not collected.

Finally, two small fragments of hollow black rubber balls or bulbs and a single recent electrical fuse round out the miscellaneous artifact category.

Table 6. Miscellaneous artifacts from the Tubac testing project

	Slag	Cinders	Concrete	Burned Adobe	Rubber	Electrical	Total
Feature 1	-	-	-	-	1	-	1
Feature 2	8	-	1	6	-	-	14
Feature 3	3	-	1	-	-	-	4
Feature 4	49	64	-	-	-	-	113
Feature 5	1	-	-	-	-	-	1
Feature 6	3	-	-	-	-	-	3
Trench 2	-	-	-	2	-	-	2
Trench 6	-	-	-	-	-	1	1
Trench 10	-	-	1	-	1	-	2
Total	64	64	3	8	2	1	142

Nonartifactual Material

This category of specimens consists of those objects that have not been fashioned by man but are the result of his use of resources. In the case of the Tubac testing project, this category contains animal bone, a single marine shell fragment, and a few pieces of wood. The wood was found in the northern end of Trench 1 and was noted but not collected. It represented a heavy square post and may have been part of the backstop for the baseball diamond associated with the school (Leland Crawford, personal communication).

Animal Bone

Bones and bone fragments were commonly encountered in both the backhoe trenches and the features uncovered during the testing. The animal bone received only a preliminary analysis. Those specimens sufficiently intact were identified as to which bone they represented and, insofar as possible, which species they represented. Most of the specimens recovered from the testing were small fragments of long bone shafts--these were recorded as scrap.

The identification of bones to the species level was complicated by the presence of both sheep and goat remains, particularly in Feature 4. Despite fairly distinctive external appearances, the two animals are extremely close skeletally, and it is often difficult to separate the two (Boessneck 1970). As a result, while the presence of both goats and sheep was verified for Feature 4, a larger number of specimens could only be identified as goat/sheep (Table 7). A similar problem was encountered with fragments of bones that were clearly derived from an animal larger than a goat or sheep; such undiagnostic specimens were listed only as cow/horse. Similar problems were noted by Hewitt (1975) in his analysis of the bone from the presidio excavations. Table 7 lists the various species identified from the testing, and Table 8 presents the numbers of pieces of bone from the trenches and features.

Most of the features and trenches produced only one or two pieces of bone sufficiently intact to identify; usually they contained only scrap. However, Feature 4 yielded the majority of the bone (57.5 percent), and nearly all of the bone sufficiently complete to identify to species and element came from this feature (Tables 7 and 8). Level 3, below the ash lens, produced most of this bone, as noted earlier. Some interesting differences are evident between Level 2 and 3, and these may be used to infer a change in function of Feature 4 at some point in time. In Levels 1 and 2 there were few identifiable pieces of bone; most of it was scrap. Scrap composed 98.7 percent of the bone from Level 1, and 91.9 percent of the bone from Level 2. In addition, approximately one-third of the bone scrap from Levels 1 and 2 was heavily burned to a white or bluish black color. However, in Level 3 only 66.1 percent of the bone was scrap, and only 0.03 percent of it was burned. Level 3 yielded far more large pieces

Table 7. Animal species represented in the Tubac testing project

	Capra hircus (Goat)	Ovis aries (Sheep)	Capra/Ovis (Goat/Sheep)	Bos sp. (Cow)	Equus caballus (Horse)	Canis sp. (Dog or Coyote)	Gallus gallus (Chicken)	Bos/Equus (Cow/Horse)
Feature 1			X					
Feature 2				X				
Feature 3							X	
Feature 4	X	X	X	X		X		X
Feature 5								X
Trench 1				X				
Trench 2				X	X			

Table 8. Quantities of animal bone recovered from the Tubac testing project

	Features					Trenches					Total
	1	2	3	4	5	1	2	6	10	17	
Pieces of Bone	13	72	172	449	23	18	14	1	7	12	781

of bone that could be identified as to element, and four separate species (Capra hircus, Ovis aries, Bos sp., and Canis sp.) were recognized. Most of the identifiable bone represented goats (Capra hircus), with some sheep (Ovis aries), and many elements could have been either goats or sheep. Of additional significance is the fact that most of the sheep, goat, and cow (Bos sp.) bones that were identifiable represented "trash" bones, those portions of the animal that contain little or no useful meat. Such elements as metapodials, distal tibiae, vertebrae, carpal/tarsal elements, and part of the cranium were most common. In addition, many of the larger limb bones in Level 3 had been split open, possibly for extraction of the marrow.

These data suggest that Feature 4 initially served as a dump for the butchered remains of carcasses, the useless residue from slaughtering. At this time the pit was apparently open and relatively deep, and the bone deposited in it received little or no damage after it was deposited. After the pit had filled to a considerable extent, the ash lens material came to be deposited, including a number of small bone fragments, some of which were heavily burned. This period of use appears to reflect the dumping of household or fireplace cleanings as noted earlier, including small fragments of meat cut bone but no whole elements or even large pieces. This implies that slaughtering and butchering were no longer being performed on the spot. Level 1 contains far less ash but more domestic trash (ceramics, glass, etc.) and the same sorts of tiny bone fragments.

Features 1, 2, 3, and 5 contained bone that was most similar to that present in Levels 1 and 2 of Feature 4. That is, the bone from these features tended to be rather badly weathered and eroded. Feature 6 yielded no bone.

Shell

Feature 2 yielded a single fragment of a marine shell that was identified as representing the genus Turritella. Such shells probably have their origins in the Gulf of California, and may be from either prehistoric or historic contexts in the Southwest.

Management Recommendations

The testing operations have shown that buried archaeological features are present in both Locus A and Locus B in addition to the wall footings visible on the surface in both loci. Furthermore, hand-dug test pits and trenches suggest that although two of the wall footings (Features 9 and 10) retain little to no archaeological research potential, many of the buried features appear to contain information of value. Because these deposits are so little mixed with later (post-1885) materials, they should be of use in reconstructing and understanding life in Tubac during the

Middle, and early portion of the Late periods (1800-1885). In addition,
they could form a source of comparative material for the research already
performed at the presidio; research done in the two tested loci would be
complementary to that in the presidio area. For these reasons we
recommend that any future development plans involving the tested area
take into account the effect that such development is likely to have on
the archaeological remains documented to exist there.

The type and nature of the proposed development will in large part
dictate what may need to be done with the archaeological resources. Any
sort of development that would involve earthmoving (leveling, pipe installa-
tion, roadways, etc.) must be evaluated carefully. If it is designed to
involve areas where archaeological features exist and is likely to affect
these features, mitigative action in the form of excavation may be
necessary. On the other hand, if development is proposed that would not
involve earthmoving (picnic areas, pedestrian trails, interpretive signs,
etc.) and would not directly affect the archaeological resources, no
further mitigative work may be needed. It should be noted that one feature,
the shallow trash pit designated Feature 3, is extremely susceptible to
impact due to its position near the surface; it also has been shown to
contain important information. It is recommended that it be excavated in
the event of any proposed development of Locus B.

In summary, any proposed developments in the tested area should be
carefully planned by the State Parks Board in consultation with the State
Historic Preservation Office. The Cultural Resource Management Division of
the Arizona State Museum will be pleased to aid in this process as well.

References

Barnes, Mark R., and Ronald V. May
   1972   Mexican majolica in northern New Spain. Pacific Coast
           Archaeological Society Occasional Paper 2. Costa Mesa,
           CA.

Bents, Doris W.
   1949   The history of Tubac, 1752-1948. Ms., master's thesis,
           University of Arizona, Tucson.

Boessneck, J.
   1970   Osteological differences between sheep (Ovis aries Linné)
           and goat (Capra hircus Linné). In Science in Archaeology,
           edited by Don Brothwell and Eric Higgs, pp. 331-58; New
           York: Praeger Publishers.

Brinckerhoff, Sidney B., and Pierce A. Chamberlain
   1972   Spanish Military Weapons in Colonial America 1700-1821.
           Harrisburg: Stackpole Books.

Browne, J. Ross
   1869   Adventures in the Apache Country: A Tour Through Arizona and
           Sonora With Notes on the Silver Regions of Nevada. New York:
           Harper Brothers.

Conklin, E.
   1878   Picturesque Arizona. New York: The Mining Record Printing
           Establishment.

DiPeso, Charles C.
   1953   The Sobaipuri Indians of the upper San Pedro River Valley,
           southeastern Arizona. Dragoon: The Amerind Foundation 6.

Dobyns, Henry F.
   1959   Tubac through four centuries, an historical resumé and
           analysis. Ms. Arizona State Museum, University of Arizona,
           Tucson.

Fontana, Bernard L. and W.J. Robinson, C.W. Cormack, and E.E. Leavitt,
   1962   Jr. Papago Indian Pottery. Seattle: University of
           Washington Press.

Gerald, Rex E.
   1968   Spanish presidios of the late eighteenth century in
           northern New Spain. Museum of New Mexico Research Records
           7. Museum of New Mexico, Santa Fe.

Haury, Emil W.
   1950   The Stratigraphy and Archaeology of Ventana Cave, Arizona.
           Tucson: University of Arizona Press. Albuquerque:
           University of New Mexico Press.

Hewitt, James M.
  1975   The faunal archaeology of the Tubac Presidio. Appendix in
          Excavations at the Tubac Presidio, by Lynette O. Shenk and
          George A. Teague, Arizona State Museum Archaeological
          Series 85.

Hinton, Richard J.
  1954   The Handbook to Arizona. Tucson: Arizona Silhouettes.

Lister, Florence C., and Robert H. Lister
  1975   Non-Indian ceramics from the Mexico City subway. El
          Palacio 81(2):25-48.

McHenry, Paul Graham, Jr.
  1973   Adobe-Build it Yourself. Tucson: University of Arizona
          Press.

North, Diane M.T.
  1980   Samuel Peter Heintzelman and the Sonora Exploring and Mining
          Company. Tucson: University of Arizona Press.

Robinson, William J.
  1976   Mission Guevavi: excavations in the convento. The Kiva
          42(2): 135-175.

Shenk, Lynette O., and George A. Teague
  1975   Excavations at the Tubac Presidio. Arizona State Museum
          Archaeological Series 85.

Toulouse, Julian H.
  1971   Bottle Makers and Their Marks. New York: Thomas Nelson,
          Inc.

Tunnell, Curtis
  1966   A description of enameled earthenware from an archaeologi-
          cal excavation at Mission San Antonio de Velero (the Alamo)
          State Building Commission Archaeological Program Report
          2. Austin.

CHAPTER 5

AN ARCHAEOLOGICAL INVESTIGATION OF AZ BB:13:146,
A SMALL OCCUPATION SITE IN THE TUCSON BASIN,
PIMA COUNTY, ARIZONA

by

Allen Dart and James Gibb

with contributions by

Charles H. Miksicek
Suzanne K. Fish

for

Pulte Home Corporation,
Tucson, Arizona

The Cultural Resource Management Division
Arizona State Museum
University of Arizona

July 1981

Table of Contents

List of Figures

List of Tables

Abstract

Archaeological investigations of a small Rincon Phase occupation site in Tucson, Arizona are reported. AZ BB:13:146 contained a single pit house ruin, an exterior hearth, and a sparse surface scatter of artifacts. The results of an archaeological testing program and a subsequent excavation are discussed, and excavation results are interpreted.

Acknowledgments

The Pulte Home Corporation generously provided funding for the archaeological survey, testing program, and subsequent excavations of features at AZ BB:13:146, as well as additional funds for laboratory analyses. Extra funding was volunteered after it was discovered that subsurface features at the site exceeded expectations based on the original survey and testing programs. Mr. Terry Klipp was most helpful in arranging grants beyond amounts specified in the original contract, and to him and the other officials of Pulte Home Corporation we are most grateful.

For working in temperatures exceeding 100° F in June, with no complaints and with commendable enthusiasm, thanks are due crew members who participated in the excavation: James Gibb, Michael H. Bartlett, Ron Gardiner, Susan A. Brew, and Ben Smith. James Gibb and Barbara Hall had done the earlier studies on the site.

The laboratory of the Salt-Gila Aqueduct Archaeological Project arranged their scheduling to allow cleaning of artifacts collected from AZ BB:13:146, and Bruce B. Huckell of the Cultural Resource Management Division took time out from his work to examine and comment on the artifacts. I am again indebted to Bruce for identifying pottery types with which I am not familiar. Charles H. Miksicek and Suzanne K. Fish analyzed flotation and pollen samples from the site and compiled reports. All these folks are gratefully acknowledged.

Finally, I would like to thank Susan Brew for again giving me an opportunity to work in southern Arizona.

Introduction

AZ BB:13:146 was a small archaeological site located just inside the eastern city limits of Tucson in Pima County, Arizona (Figure 1). It was situated in the NW 1/4 of the NE 1/4, Section 11, T14S, R15E, at Universal Transverse Mercator coordinates E518180, N3545230 (Zone 12). The site was comprised primarily of a Hohokam pit house which had burned, leaving an intact artifact assemblage in place at the floor level. Also present were an exterior hearth or roasting pit and a widely dispersed scatter of surface artifacts including a projectile point apparently dating to the Archaic Period.

Site Situation and Environment

The site was situated on geologically recent alluvial deposits which have been terraced and dissected. The dissection has resulted in the formation of four fingerlike ridges trending north from the main terrace which borders the southern portion of the project area (Figure 2). Three of these ridges have well-developed caliche formations with smooth upper surfaces. The westernmost ridge has very little caliche development. The ridge surfaces are capped by a fairly homogeneous pea-sized gravel and sand mixture.

The ridge slopes descend gradually to the north where they terminate in a small bench area overlooking an intermittent stream. The bench area is composed of sand and well-rounded, pea-sized gravel mixed with occasional small, angular fragments of caliche. This deposit averages about 1.5 m in thickness. It is underlain by a siltier zone. The gravel and sand matrix of the bench area is slightly indurated, homogeneous, and brown in color, with more organic inclusions than that of the ridges above the bench.

The intermittent stream runs northeast through the project area and joins a northwest-trending channel just north of East Speedway Boulevard (Figure 2). From that point, the wash continues northward for approximately one kilometer where it joins Tanque Verde Wash. The age of the streambed is undetermined, but considerable erosion and redeposition evidently has occurred in this area through time.

Vegetation in the site area is dominated by creosote-bush with lesser amounts of palo-verde, mesquite, and perennial grasses distributed evenly throughout. The banks of the intermittent stream running through the project area contain thick stands of mesquite, to the near exclusion of all other species.

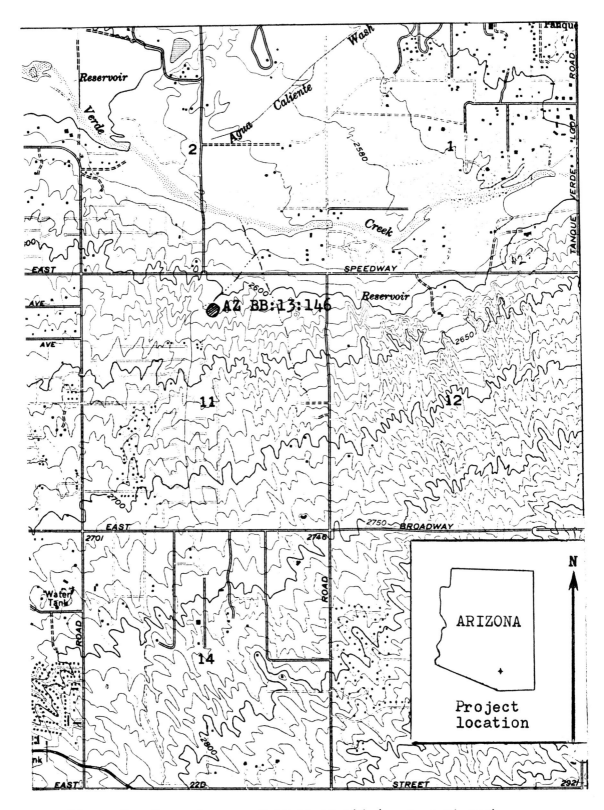

Figure 1. General area of AZ BB:13:146 (scale 1:24,000)

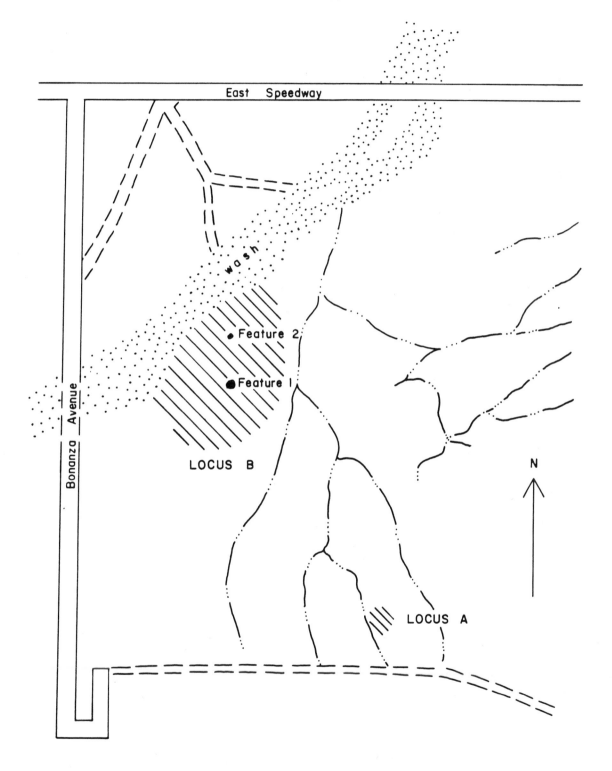

Figure 2. Location of AZ BB:13:146

Site History and Previous Investigations

AZ BB:13:146 was first recorded in March, 1981, by Arizona State Museum (ASM) archaeologist Barbara Hall during an archaeological clearance survey of a 40-acre parcel of land targeted for development by the Pulte Home Corporation. (Due to an incorrect recording procedure, the site at that time was designated AZ BB:13:138. This designation was listed in the original survey report and the subsequent testing phase report. This number has since been changed in the Arizona State Museum site files, because AZ BB:13:138 was assigned in the files to a different site. The correct designation for the site of this study is AZ BB:13:146.) Hall reported the site as a thin scatter of prehistoric pottery fragments spread over a large area of more than 120,000 square meters (30± acres). Due to difficulty in predicting the extent of any possible subsurface cultural materials in such a situation, ASM recommended that this site undergo subsurface testing to determine its depth, extent, significance, and eligibility for inclusion on the State and/or National Register of Historic Places.

The testing recommendation was accepted by Pulte Home Corporation, and additional funds were provided for such a program. Therefore, sub-surface testing and surface sampling operations were conducted from June 1 through 4, 1981 by ASM archaeologists James Gibb and Barbara Hall. During that project, two areas were identified which were thought to have potential to yield primary cultural deposits: the ridge tops and the bench area.

The easternmost ridge top was designated Locus A, and the low bench on the northwest portion of the site was designated Locus B. These two loci were gridded, mapped, and collected. Subsurface testing was then conducted in the two loci and in areas atop the other two ridges in the vicinity. Twelve backhoe trenches were excavated, one in Locus A, six in Locus B, and five in the area between the two loci. Only two trenches, both in Locus B, revealed remains of subsurface cultural features. In Trench 9, a stratum containing pottery and a high charcoal-ash content was designated Feature 1. In Trench 12, a pit filled with cobbles and fine ash was designated Feature 2. Feature 1 was tentatively identified as the remains of a pit house. Feature 2 was tentatively identified as a hearth.

An Archaic tradition projectile point (Figure 4a) was the only artifact recovered during testing operations that suggested any human activity in the area earlier than the Rincon Phase of the Hohokam tradition sequence in the Tucson Basin. This point was found on the surface, and its relative isolation at the site and the nature of an impact fracture at the tip suggested to Gibb and Hall (1981:7) that it was lost while hunting was occurring in the area.

The point is of pink chert or rhyolite, and in size and form is similar to the triangular, concave-based points found by Cattanach

(1966:16) at a San Pedro Stage site near Fairbank, Arizona. Cattanach's points in this category averaged 38 mm long (unbroken), 20 mm wide, and 8 mm thick. Leaf-shaped and convex-based points were also found at that site, in association with diagnostic, stemmed, San Pedro Stage points. Haury (1975:275) notes rather similar points at Ventana Cave and postulates that they may be a late refinement of the leaf-shaped points. Huckell (1980:120-172) located similar points during testing operations in the Rosemont area of the Santa Rita Mountains southeast of Tucson, in the context of one lithic scatter and one sherd-and-lithic scatter. Huckell notes that two other preceramic sites in that general area also have such points, and cites other examples in the literature. No absolute dates are available, however, from the context of these various finds. Huckell concludes that they are a late Archaic tradition manifestation. As the point at AZ BB:13:146 is a surface find, it cannot yield an absolute date either. It is reasonable to suggest, however, a late Archaic manufacture date for it on typological grounds.

All other artifacts recovered from AZ BB:13:146 during the testing project were pieces of broken pottery. The surface-collection ceramics appear to be of Rincon Phase age. The majority are local plain wares ranging in color from tan to brownish red, with occasional fire-clouding. A very few plain brown sherds exhibit possible deliberate interior smuding (a late Rincon trait). All sherds possess a sand temper with varying micaceous content.

The four sherds collected from the surface of Locus A appear to be from one vessel. These are plain, jar-body sherds, reddish brown in color with a blackened interior. The ceramic collection from the surface of Locus B mainly consists of sherds from local plain ware jars. There are a few bowl sherds as well. Three sherds of a Rincon Red-on-brown jar were also found at Locus B, and the exclusively angular decoration on these may indicate manufacture during the late Rincon Phase (Greenleaf 1975:60). Also found on the surface at Locus B were one slightly corroded red ware bowl sherd, a plain ware Gila shoulder section from a jar, a tiny piece of a straight-sided, flat-topped rim, probably from a jar but too small to identify for certain, and an interior-smudged bowl sherd with red line decoration.

It was concluded from examination of the pottery types that the Hohokam component of AZ BB:13:146 probably dated to either the late Rincon or early Cortaro Phase (approximately A.D. 1100 to 1200) of the Tucson Basin chronology, and that Feature 1 (the pit house) was associated with the Hohokam occupation. If such a date is correct, it may indicate that the site was related to a larger site, AZ BB:13:68, located a few hundred meters to the east and occupied during both the Rincon and later Tanque Verde Phases.

No date was assigned to Feature 2 (the exterior hearth) due to lack of associated artifacts, but it was suggested that the depth of the feature, which was greater than the depth of the pit house, plus the presence of an Archaic-style projectile point at the site, might indicate the presence of a late Archaic tradition component at AZ BB:13:146.

It was recommended by ASM that further archaeological investigations of the two features be undertaken before development began on the property.

Excavation Project Organization

Pulte Home Corporation agreed to a proposal of further archaeological investigations by ASM archaeologists. Consequently, three days were spent in the field excavating and mapping the two features.

The excavation project was supervised by Allen Dart. Others who worked during the investigation were James Gibb, Michael H. Bartlett, Ron Gardiner, Susan A. Brew, and Ben Smith. During the first two days (June 20 and 21, 1981), Dart and Gibb worked primarily on Feature 1, with Brew aiding in mapping the feature. On June 29, all the excavators, except Gibb, completed excavation of both Features 1 and 2. Approximately 60 person-hours were spent in field operations during the excavation phase.

Research Questions Guiding Investigations

Given the apparently limited nature of AZ BB:13:146, investigations were conducted with only a few specific research questions in mind.

First, what was the extent of the pit house?

Second, what was the context of this feature; that is, what was it used for in a topographic area seemingly unsuited to large-scale agricultural pursuits?

Third, what was the date of this structure? It was hoped a more secure date could help establish whether, in fact, this site was associated temporally with AZ BB:13:68 to the east. Consequently, special attention was paid to collecting as much datable material as possible from floor associations within the structure.

Finally, we wished to try to establish whether or not the exterior hearth was contemporaneous with the pit house, whether there was any indication of its use earlier, and what it might have been used for.

Data Recovery Strategy

Our primary objective in information recovery was to obtain as much data as possible in the limited amount of time available to us. No machine excavation equipment was available to remove overburden from either feature, so excavation began with shoveling off the overburden of Feature 1 to an arbitrary level about 10 cm above where the probable house floor had been seen in the sides of Trench 9. All artifacts observed while shovling were collected without maintaining any particular locational controls except depth. Grid stakes which had been placed over the feature during the testing project were re-used for mapping purposes, although new coordinate designations were given to the stakes for easier reference (Figure 3). Due to limited time and manpower, the excavated dirt was tossed onto the previously back-filled Trench 9 area and beyond it to the east. This made excavation of any portion of the pit house east of the trench very impractical. Fortunately, there was little possibility that the structural limits extended beyond the edge of that trench (Figure 3). Smaller amounts of excavated dirt were placed north and south of where the structural limits were believed to be, until the actual limits were better defined.

After a common level was obtained over most of the area where the structure was thought to be, two test excavations were made away from Trench 9 to determine where the floor level actually was. A small pit was excavated with trowel in the southwestern portion of the house area until a dramatic change in color from charcoal-stained fill to an unstained, light-brown soil was recognized, similar to what had been observed earlier in the backhoe trench sides. Meanwhile, a shovel-width trench was dug running westward from the backhoe trench to the same level.

Once the floor level was established, excavation of the fill from 0 cm to 10 cm above the floor was begun using shovels, scraping down gradually until either the floor level or artifacts were encountered. When artifacts were seen, trowel excavation began in order to preserve the associational context of the artifacts with the structure itself and with other artifacts. A 6-mm mesh screen was used only when removing dirt from around substantial concentrations of artifacts. Using the combination of shoveling and troweling, the entire floor area was gradually exposed. Artifacts were mapped as they were discovered, then immediately removed and bagged (a few, such as broken vessels or larger clusters of several artifacts, were photographed in place before they were removed). Pollen and flotation samples were collected from beneath a large cluster of broken jar sherds, and separate flotation samples were collected from various places in the above-floor fill, especially from areas rich in charcoal.

After larger portions of the floor level had been exposed by scraping, this surface was swept to reveal any possible subfloor features such as pits. When two such features were found, they were excavated with trowels. All the fill dirt was saved for flotation and pollen analyses.

In excavating Feature 2, the plan was to remove the dirt which had been used to back-fill the backhoe trench, relocate the hearth feature in the re-exposed trench site, then remove the overlying fill before

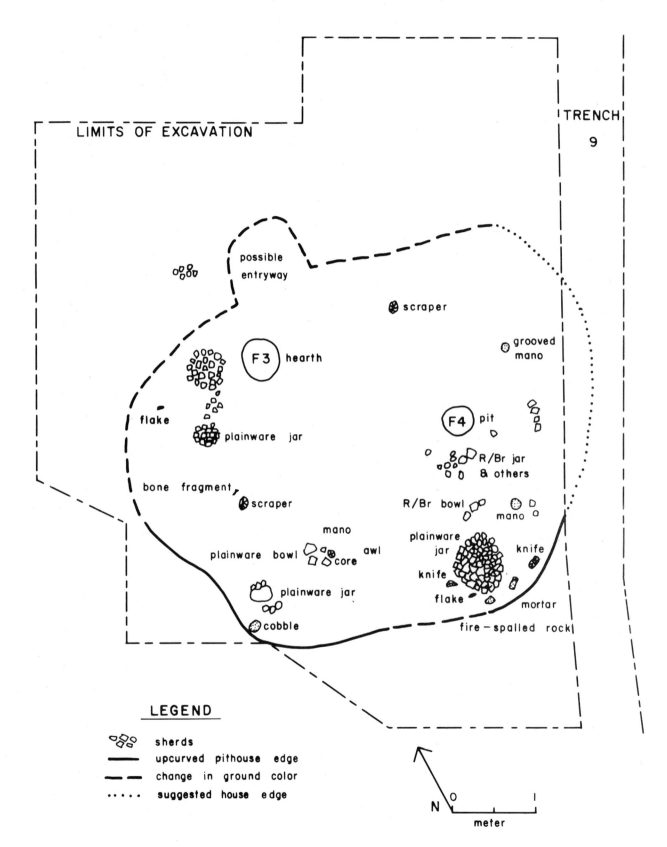

Figure 3.   AZ BB:13:146, Feature 1 floor plan

excavating it by hand. Unfortunately, the trench side containing the feature evidently had collapsed while the trench was being back-filled, destroying Feature 2.

Excavation Results

No usable information was recovered from the isolated hearth, Feature 2. Discussion therefore will center on the data recovered from the pit house ruin, Feature 1. In brief, this structure was excavated slightly into the sloping ground surface, contained an interior hearth (designated Feature 3), and one subfloor pit (designated Feature 4), and had an extensive artifact and stored food assemblage in place when it was destroyed by fire. The structure, the artifacts and their distributions, and information on plant remains and environmental implications are discussed below.

Architecture

Feature 1 was not particularly well preserved due to very extensive rodent burrowing in the fill and beneath the floor. Rodent activity had been so extensive, in fact, that a strong odor of ammonia and other urine derivatives made excavating unpleasant. The rodent disturbances caused most of the pit house area to be poorly defined. Rodents were also responsible for the scattering of artifacts from the locations where they had been abandoned.

The degree of burrowing through the floor may have destroyed or obscured any interior posts which might have been present; in any event, no interior posts were defined. The western and northern limits of the structure were defined by a continuous black stain at the floor level, and this stain is almost certainly the result of what once had been a line of posts. The southwestern and southern limits showed no evidence of any posts, suggesting that this side of the structure had not burned as intensively prior to collapse of the structure. The lack of definite postholes is most probably attributable, however, to the nature of the earth into which the structure had been built. The alluvium of the general area of the site was comprised mainly of coarse sand and small gravels which would have quickly collapsed into any cavity left by a deteriorated post.

Feature 1 measured 4.4 m north-south by an estimated 5.8 m east-west (the eastern edge of the house had been removed by the backhoe when Trench 9 was dug). Floor area was estimated at 20.09 square meters, exclusive of a possible entryway on the north side (Figure 3). This likely entryway was a vague extension of the darker-colored interior house fill beyond the black-stained northern limit of the house. It was bulbous in shape and measured 1.0 m east-west by 0.7 m north-south. Its area was estimated to be 0.64 square meters. The house was shaped like an irregular oval.

Evidently the pit house had been dug only partially into the sloping alluvial surface, just enough to help level the floor surface. The northern portion of the floor level was flush with the original exterior surface, while the southern portion was cut into the slope an average of about 12 cm. Even with this attempt at leveling, the southern area of the floor was about 8 cm higher than the northern area. Therefore, the entryway on the northern side (if it was an entryway) was at the same level as the house floor in that area.

The nature of construction of the upper structure of the house remains undetermined due to the lack of postholes found. However, it may be surmised that it was built of cottonwood and foothills palo-verde, and probably also incorporated mesquite, blue palo-verde, and graythorn twigs (Appendix 1).

A shallow, elliptical pit centered 0.7 m south of the northern house limit and near the supposed entryway was probably the remnant of a hearth. This hearth (Feature 3) was 0.42 m north-south by 0.36 m east-west and 0.10 m deep. There was no evidence that it had been plastered, but it contained a small amount of fine charcoal and ash. A second, deeper pit (Feature 4) was situated in the east-central portion of the house. It measured 0.26 m north-south by 0.33 m east-west at the mouth, and extended 0.32 m below the floor level of the house. This pit would have been mistaken for a posthole except for the large amount of burned corn contained in it, indicating it was used for storage. The burned material was only found in the upper 20 cm of fill, suggesting stored food caught fire when the house burned, and that the combustion did not penetrate all the way to the pit bottom.

The floor itself was only visible as a change in color. There was no plastering evident, and the color contrast consisted of black-stained fill above the floor level, with the regular beige alluvium beneath that level. Most of the artifacts found in Feature 1 were distributed at about this level, varying somewhat due to rodent disturbance. The color change and the artifacts made definition of the floor level fairly easy. Several artifacts were found on the floor.

Artifacts

Artifacts recovered from excavation at AZ BB:13:146, besides the pottery, lithics, and projectile point found during the earlier archaeological testing operations, include pottery, manos, a small mortar, tabular knives, lithic debitage and flaked stone tools, and a bone awl fragment. A descriptive summary of the artifacts follows, and discussion of the implications of the assemblage is presented in the Conclusions.

Ceramics

Only three formal pottery types were identified among the sherds recovered from excavation of Feature 1, but there were the remains of at least 11 vessels. The pottery types were identified by Bruce B. Huckell of the Arizona State Museum as Rincon Red-on-brown, Rincon Red, and untyped plain ware indigenous to the Tucson Basin. A few examples of unidentified red-on-brown sherds were present, and many of the other sherds had surfaces too worn to permit identification. The unidentified sherds have been lumped together with the plain wares in the following analyses.

The pottery from AZ BB:13:146 typically contains muscovite mica and coarse, rounded sand in the temper. Some fire-clouding was present on a few of the plain ware pieces, and the surface finish varied from relatively smooth to very rough in the large jar interiors. Jar exteriors and bowl interiors were all relatively smooth.

The design styles on the Rincon Red-on-brown vessels are quite characteristic of the Rincon Phase. They show little indication of design elements transitional to earlier or later phases (Figure 4b, 4c).

Table 1 summarizes the counts, weights, and percentage of total ceramic assemblage weight of all the ceramics recovered during excavation of Feature 1. By weight, plain wares form the great bulk of the assemblage, although it should be noted that the "plain or unidentifiable" category most likely contains some sherds which were parts of the decorated vessels. However, the 94 percent plain ware figure is probably close to the actual percentage, since most of the plain ware vessel rims were from very large, heavy jars, while the decorated pottery vessels were much finer, smaller bowls and jars. Table 2 shows the number of vessels of the various types: there were at least seven plain ware vessels, three red-on-brown, and one red ware container. The minimum number of jars and bowls was calculated from different design styles and presence of decoration as well as rim form on the painted ware, and simply by rim form on the plain and red ware items.

Remains of two Rincon Red-on-brown bowls and one Rincon Red-on-brown jar were found. In each case, probably between 20 and 50 percent of the vessel was recovered. The lack of completeness of each vessel (each found in an on-floor context) can probably be attributed to the extensive rodent disturbances which characterized the fill and floor levels of the pit house. The two bowls were distinguished by the different design patterns (Figures 4b, 4c) present. Rincon Red-on-brown Bowl "A" (Figure 4b) was fairly scattered after it was broken. Its sherds were found in various places on the house floor and in the fill. Rincon Red-on-brown Bowl "B" (Figure 4c) sherds were all clustered together in the southeastern portion of the house (Figure 3), but only about half of this vessel remained in place. The third Rincon Red-on-brown vessel was a jar, and its sherds were all located beside a subfloor pit in the house (Figure 3).

Figure 4. Artifacts from AZ BB:13:146: a) Archaic tradition
projectile point; b) Rincon Red-on-brown "Bowl A" design pattern;
c) Rincon Red-on-brown "Bowl B" design pattern

Table   1.   Ceramics associated with Feature 1, AZ BB:13:146

Types	Count	Weight (gm)	Weight % of Total Assemblage
Rincon Red-on-brown	34	858	5.4
Unidentified Red-on-brown	7	64	0.4
Rincon Red	3	36	0.2
Plain or Unidentified	609	15,047	94.0
Total	653	16,005	100.0

Table   2.   Types and numbers of vessels associated with Feature 1, AZ BB:13:146

Pottery Type	Vessel Type	Minimum Number of Vessels
Rincon Red-on-brown	Bowl	2
Rincon Red-on-brown	Jar	1
Rincon Red	Bowl ?	1
Plain	Bowl	2
Plain	Jar	5

Three sherds of Rincon Red were found. The small rim sherd of this type suggests that there was at least one steep-sided bowl of red ware, which made up less than 1 percent of the total ceramic assemblage. Remains of Rincon Red were found in a small sherd cluster on the northern exterior of the house (Figure 3) and in the general fill.

Remains of two plain ware bowls and at least five plain ware jars were found in Feature 1. The bowls were of two styles, Style "A" with a direct rim and Style "B" with a lipped rim (Figure 5a, 5b). Several sherds of Style A were collected, one of which had a drilled mend-hole near one of the broken edges. A few of the Style A bowl sherds were found in a cluster on the floor in the southwest quadrant of the house, and the rest in fill. The only example of a Style B bowl rim was found in general floor fill from the western side of the room.

Plain ware jar rims had four separate forms (Figure 5c-5e). Two of the jars were of Jar Style A, the form in Figure 5c, distinguished from one another by different extrapolations of outside rim diameters (23 cm and 27 cm). The other three jars were all of different rim forms (Figure 5d-5f). Remains of the larger diameter Style A jar were concentrated in the southeast quadrant of the house, and those of the smaller one in the northwest quadrant (Figure 3). The single example of a Style B jar rim was found in a cluster of plain ware sherds in the southwest quadrant of the house (Figure 3). Rims of the smaller jar Styles C and D (Figure 5e, 5f) were both found in general fill context, suggesting they may have been part of a roof artifact assemblage.

Ground Stone

Ground stone artifacts found in Feature 1 include three manos, one cobble pounding tool, a cylindrical mortar, and two tabular knives. All these items were found on the house floor.

Two of the manos are quartzite stream cobbles exhibiting pecking or grinding on nearly every exposure. Both have smooth-ground surfaces on two sides, worn in a rocking, back-and-forth motion. The pecking does not seem to have been intended to reshape the overall form of either stone, but rather to roughen the portions not used for grinding. The smaller mano (11.6 cm by 11.1 cm by 6.6 cm) was found in the southeast quadrant of the house; the larger one (14.2 cm by 13.4 cm by 6.3 cm) was located in the south central portion (Figure 3). The larger mano was heat-cracked all the way around its circular edge.

A biscuit-shaped mano of pink quartzite (Figure 6b) was found in the eastern portion of the room (Figure 3). This artifact is slightly elliptical, measuring 8.5 cm by 8.0 cm by 4.6 cm thick. A shallow groove encircling the stone was probably intended to facilitate handling. This stone is similar to items found at the Snaketown Site which Haury (1976: 281-282) classifies as a variation of mano type 1b. Haury notes that

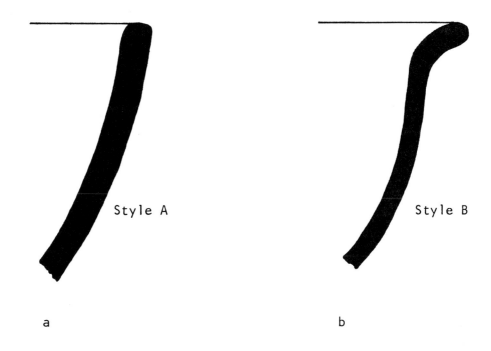

Plain ware bowls

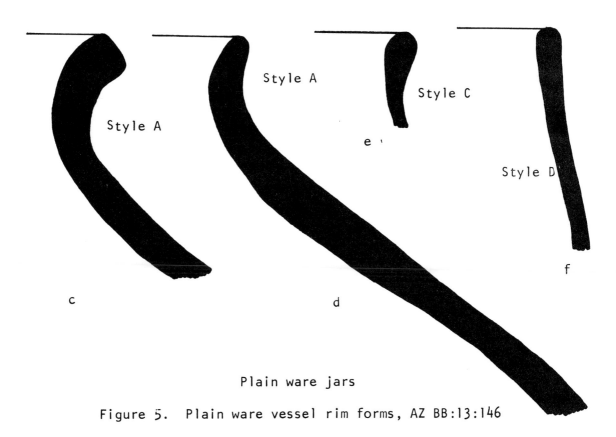

Plain ware jars

Figure 5. Plain ware vessel rim forms, AZ BB:13:146

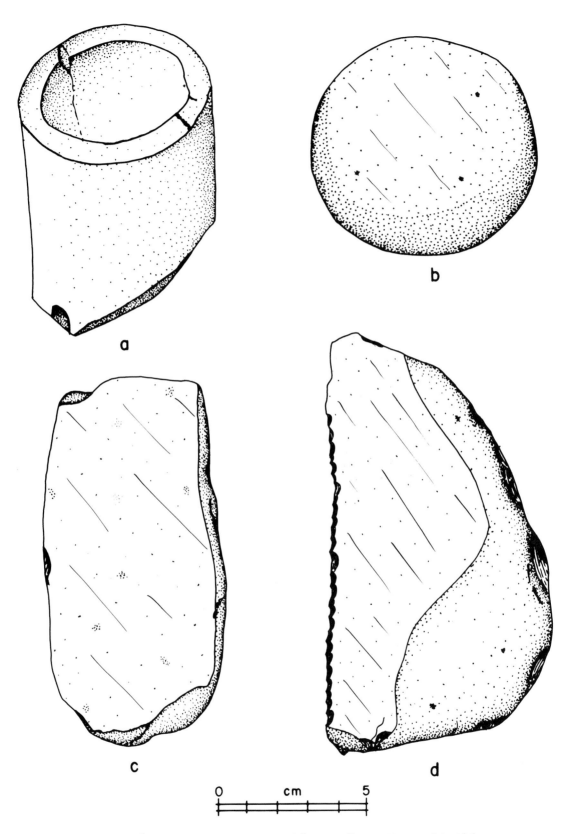

Figure 6. Ground stone artifacts from AZ BB:13:146, Feature 1 floor contact: a) mortar; b) grooved mano (oblique view); c, d) tabular knives

this variation with the "pulley effect" appears to have been limited to Sedentary and Classic Periods.

A stream cobble of granitic material was found along the southwest edge of the floor (Figure 3). This cobble measures 12.6 cm by 11.1 cm by 5.2 cm, and examination under a dissecting microscope revealed damage caused by crushing motions on the flattest portion of its surface.

The mortar (Figure 6a) is very nearly cylindrical, measuring 8.7 cm by 7.9 cm elliptically, and 8.0 cm long in the outer dimensions. The mortar hole itself measures 7.0 cm by 6.5 cm elliptically, and 1.8 cm deep. It was made from finely porphyritic basalt and is fairly well polished on the exterior sides. The bottom does not appear to have been modified, and the mortar depression shows rough crushing wear. One heat-spall was still in place when the item was found, while another spall apparently removed prior to the house fire was not present. The mortar was found along the southeastern margin of the floor (Figure 3).

Two tabular knives were found in the southeastern quadrant of the house (Figure 3). Both are of a tabular material resembling slate, but Bruce Huckell suggests the waviness of the grain in the stone indicates the material may be phyllite. The smaller of the knives (Figure 6c) is subrectangular in form, and its cross section is wedge-shaped, tapering from 11 mm on the thicker side to about 2 mm on the thinner cutting edge. The cutting edge is extremely worn, but it appears that it may have been serrated prior to extensive use. The larger knife (Figure 6d) is nearly triangular, and its straight cutting edge is serrated but also extensively worn. The sides of each of these tools are ground and polished.

Chipped Stone

Only 12 pieces of chipped stone were recovered from excavations of Feature 1. Five of the items were recovered from the general feature fill above the floor fill stratum, and the rest were in direct floor contact or in the floor fill layer among the sherds of one of the large broken jars.

For such a small chipped stone assemblage, there is quite a variety of material types represented, some of them of very good quality for chipped stone artifact manufacture. Materials include basalt, chert, chalcedony, jasper, petrified wood, and quartzite. Basalt is the most common type of material found. Material types are summarized in Table 3.

Artifact types among the chipped stone assemblage include one fairly large end-scraper, a uniface which may be a projectile point preform, two cores, and eight flakes. Five of the flakes exhibit either microscopic or macroscopic edge damage indicative of utilization.

Table 3. Chipped stone artifacts associated with Feature 1,
          AZ BB:13:146

Material Type	Scraper	Uniface (preform?)	Core	Utilized Flake	Unutilized Flake	Total
Basalt	-	-	-	4	1	5
Chert/Chalcedony	ᴸ	-	1	1	-	2
Jasper	-	1	-	-	2	3
Petrified Wood	-	-	1	-	-	1
Quartzite	1	-	-	-	-	1
Total	1	1	2	5	3	12

Bone

    Only one bone artifact, an awl fragment, was found during the excavation of Feature 1. It is made from a large mammal limb bone and measures 58 mm from the tip to the broken portion. It was found lying against the largest mano on the floor of the house, in the south central portion (Figure 3), and it was charred, probably by the same fire which destroyed the house.

Animal and Plant Remains

    While few animal remains were recovered during the excavation of AZ BB:13:146, a good deal of information was recovered concerning plant materials. This may be partially due to collection methods used during excavation: since screening was generally not done, fewer animal bones than might be expected were recovered. On the other hand, several samples of soil were taken for recovery of preserved plant materials, including pollen. A brief summary of recovered biotic materials is presented here.

Discussions of the materials are presented in the Conclusions and in the Appendixes.

Bone

The only animal remains recovered during the project were two pieces of mammal bone. One of these was the large mammal awl fragment discussed above. The other was a large mammal bone fragment found on the floor in the west-central portion of the house. The awl fragment was made from a limb bone, but the body part of the other fragment could not be determined due to its small size. Both pieces were burned, probably during the house conflagration.

Burned Plant Materials

Five flotation samples were collected for examination of carbonized plant materials. One sample (SN 1) was taken from the general fill stratum, two (SN 4 and 5) from the floor fill stratum, and one each from the hearth (SN 3) and subfloor pit (SN 2). Sample numbers (SN) 1 and 4 were assembled by collecting dirt from various places within the fill inside the pit house limits, while SN 5 came from the ash concentration which had been designated Feature 5 (evidently a natural concentration). The hearth and pit samples consisted of the entire contents of those features excepting only small amounts kept separate for pollen samples.

Details of flotation analyses are presented in Appendix A. SN 1 and 5 contained no charcoal, and few nonwood remains. Isolated pieces of blue palo-verde and desert willow charcoal were found in the floor fill, and the main house fill sample (SN 4) contained three kinds of corn and evidence of common beans and pigweed seeds, and charcoal of cottonwood and foothills palo-verde. The hearth fill sample was similar to SN 4, containing no cottonwood charcoal but also containing some grass stems. The subfloor pit contained the largest amount of burned plant remains, including charcoal of five tree or shrub species plus pigweed seeds and two types of corn.

Pollen

Three pollen samples were collected. One sample (SN 7) was taken from the general floor fill layer and consisted of pinches of dirt from various places in the eastern half of the house. The other two samples (SN 8 and 9) were taken from the hearth and subfloor pit fill.

Details of the pollen analyses are presented in Appendix B. In addition to corn pollen, pollen of another possible cultigen, Cucurbita sp. was present in the pit house floor fill layer. The general pollen indications are of an agriculturally-disturbed environment associated with the house, evident by very high levels of Cheno-Am and composites. The high levels of Cheno-Am types is comparable to modern Papago field pollen studies (Lytle-Webb 1978: Figure 5; Miksicek and Fish 1981), and their prominence is predictable in desert floodplain situations (Hevly, Mehringer and Yocum 1965; Martin 1963; Schoenwetter and Doerschlag 1971). Cattail (Typha) pollen found in both Features 3 and 4 in combination with the cottonwood charcoal in the flotation remains suggests a permanently damp riparian community nearby.

Two pollen types indicate probable economic use of gathered plants. Plantago pollen was present in Feature 3; the seeds of this species, called "Indian wheat," were gathered and eaten ethnographically. An anomalous frequency of Caryophyllaceae (Pink family) pollen was found on the pit house floor. A member of the plant family may have been used for medicinal purposes.

Summary and Conclusions

Excavation of features at AZ BB:13:146 recovered information sufficient to answer, at least partially, the research questions concerning the extent, environmental context, and occupation date of the house ruin at the site. The question concerning the relationship of the exterior hearth to the pit house in terms of contemporaneity and its specific use is left unanswered. The three answerable questions concerning Feature 1 break down broadly into categories of internal site organization, subsistence and environment, and dating and contemporaneity with other archaeological sites. The remaining discussion will deal with each of these categories, but first, a brief descriptive summary of the recovered information from the site is in order.

General Descriptive Summary

Excavations conducted during this project and during a preceding testing operation revealed that AZ BB:13:146 was the site of a Hohokam occupation on a limited basis during the Rincon Phase of the Tucson Basin Hohokam chronology (Greenleaf 1975: Figure b), with minimal suggestion of earlier Archaic tradition activity. The single Archaic artifact found at the site, a projectile point (Figure 4a), could have been collected elsewhere and transported to the site by the later Hohokam occupants, however, since it was found in a surface context. Subsurface investigation discovered a single pit house ruin and an exterior hearth or roasting pit. Little usable information could be recovered from the exterior hearth due to its accidental destruction, but the pit house yielded a fair sized artifact assemblage and preserved plant remains useful in reconstructing the prehistoric environment and the subsistence pattern of the site's occupants.

Internal Site Organization

The pit house (Feature 1) and the exterior hearth (Feature 2)
were situated on a low ridge near a northeast-trending arroyo. The
hearth was situated about 40 m north of the house. Backhoe trenching in
the general site area did not uncover evidence of any other subsurface
features, and most of the surface artifacts were confined to the same
ridge as the two features. This suggests that there was indeed only one
habitation feature at the site, Feature 1. It might be surmised that the
hearth and the house were made by the same people, but this could not be
demonstrated.

The hearth appears to have been a roasting pit similar to pits
used in processing wild plant foods as well as domesticated corn in other
archaeological sites. Such a function would be likely in the general
area of AZ BB:13:146, where wild resources likely to be roasted in such
a pit still abound: mesquite, cacti, and other edible wild foods cur-
rently grow in the vicinity. The possible entryway discovered attached
to the house was located along its north side, so that the entry faced
down-slope and toward the area of the exterior hearth.

Other information on internal site organization has to do with
the artifact assemblage found associated with the pit house. A limited
amount of excavation was done on the exterior of the house (Figure 3),
and only one small cluster of pottery was found outside the feature,
near the supposed entryway. The remaining artifacts were all found
within the structure. There was a slight suggestion of a small artifact
assemblage on the roof of the house when it burned and collapsed, but
only one vessel seemed likely to have been on the roof judging from artifact position in the fill of the house. The rest of the artifacts appear
to have been directly on the house floor, and their arrangement suggests
some activities that were occurring immediately prior to the house's
destruction.

A large concentration of artifacts was found in the southeast
quadrant of the house, including remains of one large plain ware jar, one
bowl and one jar of Rincon Red-on-brown pottery, two tabular knives,
a small mortar, a uniface, and a utilized basalt flake. The mortar and
stone tools suggest that perhaps some type of food processing was done
in this area, for storage or during meals. The three vessels and the
nearby subfloor pit would tend to support the idea of food preparation
for storage in the southeast quadrant of the house.

A less dense concentration of artifacts was situated in the
southwest quadrant of the house, but this, too, may have had to do
mostly with food preparation, and perhaps some hide processing as well.
Artifacts in the southwest quadrant include the large cobble mano, a
bone awl, a chalcedony pebble with only a few flakes taken off,
suggesting intended later use as a core, a plain ware bowl and a plain
ware jar, a river cobble used for pounding, and a thick flake possibly

used as a scraper. The awl, scraper, and possibly the river cobble may have been used in leather preparation, but the other artifacts again suggest food preparation in the southwest quadrant of the house.

The northwest quadrant of the house contained the hearth (Feature 3) along with the remains of at least one plain ware jar and one utilized basalt flake. Remains of maize, beans, and pigweed seeds were found in the hearth fill, suggesting these were being roasted on one or more occasions.

The northeast quadrant and the central area of the house were the locations of the fewest artifacts, suggesting these areas were kept clear for easy movement and perhaps for sleeping. The only artifacts found on the floor in these areas were the small grooved mano and the large end-scraper, located about 1.5 m away from each other and from any other artifacts.

Subsistence and Prehistoric Environment

Plant and animal remains at the site indicate a diet based on domesticated corn, beans, and possibly squash, supplemented by wild plant foods and at least a small amount of wild game. Most of the burned plant products found in the house, and especially in the subfloor pit, were shelled corn kernels, indicating that agriculture was a major pursuit of the house occupants. Three varieties of corn were found in the remains, although only two of the varieties were contained in the large flotation sample collected from the subfloor pit. Such a possible segregation of the varieties may suggest that the subfloor pit was used to store seed corn for the next planting season.

Although no evidence of any prehistoric canals or water control features has been reported for the nearby vicinity of the site, the area seems to have been well suited to akchin agriculture utilizing seasonal runoff to help water fields which were situated in and near washes. Castetter and Bell (1942:125, 144) note that the Papago used this method: "Every suitable plot of ground of this kind was utilized, and in many cases the plantings were necessarily very small," and that floodwater-dependent planting usually occurred in late June to mid-July, corresponding with the end of the annual saguaro fruit harvest. Such a situation probably was typical for the inhabitants of AZ BB:13:146 as well.

The gathering of wild plants for food is evidenced by the presence of burned pigweed seeds, Indian wheat, and high concentrations of Cheno-Am and plantain pollen types. The exterior roasting pit at the site may have been used for processing these and other wild plant resources, as well as domesticated plant products.

Dating and Contemporaneity With Other Sites

An approximate date for the occupation at AZ BB:13:146 is, at present, based solely on the ceramic types found there, types which have been considered comparable in age to similar types from the Gila Basin of Arizona (Greenleaf 1975; Kelly, Officer, and Haury 1978). Samples for carbon-dating were collected from excavations at the site, but this analysis has not been completed yet.

The pottery designs found on the Rincon Red-on-brown vessels from AZ BB:13:146 are quite comparable to those illustrated on late Rincon Phase examples from the Punta de Agua excavations, also located in the Santa Cruz River Basin near Tucson (Greenleaf 1975:60-66). Ceramics with these stylistic elements have been tentatively dated by Greenleaf (1975:12) to around A.D. 1150-1225, with the earlier date probably less secure than the later one. If this chronology is acceptable, then we may suggest that the Hohokam occupation at AZ BB:13:146 took place some time between A.D. 1100 and 1225, allowing a few years to be added to the earlier end of Greenleaf's phase chronology due to the seeming uncertainty of his transitional date from early to late Rincon Phase.

The Sedentary Period, of which the Rincon Phase was a temporal expression, saw a significant development of Hohokam culture growth in the Tucson Basin. Several large and small archaeological sites of this period have been identified in the area. The one nearest to AZ BB:13:146 was AZ BB:13:68, a few hundred meters to the east, also within the Tanque Verde Wash drainage area. This site contains artifacts along both ridge and floodplain areas, with a good deal of material indicative of a long period of occupation beginning with the Rincon Phase and continuing into the succeeding Tanque Verde Phase of the Classic Period. As with AZ BB:13:146, no physical evidence of occupation structures was visible on the surface of AZ BB:13:68, but the artifact density and distribution area are greater at AZ BB:13:68, and intrusive pottery (Mimbres Black-on-white) is present there, all suggestive of a much more extensive occupation with more varied relationships than at AZ BB:13:146. The natural inclination is to suggest that AZ BB:13:146 was related to this larger site in some way, probably as a small farming satellite area occupied by a single family group.

The pottery design styles found on vessels at AZ BB:13:146 indicate its occupants were integrated into the fairly widespread Sedentary Period social system, which Greenleaf (1975:19) suggests was integrated on an inter-community level.

APPENDIX A

HOHOKAM NUTRITION:
ARCHAEOBOTANICAL EVIDENCE FROM AZ BB:13:146

Charles H. Miksicek
Arizona State Museum and
Arid Lands Studies Program

        Several flotation samples from AZ BB:13:146 offer a unique
opportunity to reconstruct prehistoric protein-nutritional status for
the prehistoric occupants of the Tucson Basin. These samples, along
with several plant macrofossils, were collected during test excavations
of the site and analyzed at the Archaeobotanical Laboratories of Arizona
State Museum. These data are summarized in Tables 4 and 5. Maize and
bean remains were examined in detail using techniques summarized in
Miksicek (1979), Pearsall (1980), and Kaplan (1956). Results of the
maize analysis are presented in Table 6, and the beans are summarized in
Table 7.

        AZ BB:13:146 seems to be a small Rincon Phase satellite site
(possibly a farmstead) associated with nearby AZ BB:13:68, a much larger
site with a Rincon and Tanque Verde Phase occupation. The site consisted
of a pit house and several associated internal and external features,
near a small wash that drains into Tanque Verde Wash. The wood charcoal
remains from the site (Table 5) are suggestive of species associated
with mesquite bosques--mesquite, blue palo-verde, desert willow, and
graythorn (Condalia sp.). The presence of cottonwood charcoal suggests
fairly permanent water in the area (or very shallow subsurface water).

        The abundant maize kernels from the site were probably once
stored in baskets and perhaps in some of the 11 vessels recovered from
the site. Pueblo Indians and their Anasazi and Mogollon predecessors
stored maize on the cob. Castetter and Bell (1942) however, report that
the Pima and Papago usually store maize as shelled kernels in baskets or
ollas. This seems to have been true of the Hohokam also, as maize cobs
are rarely recovered from Hohokam sites except from hearths where they
were probably used as fuel. Bulk collections of Hohokam maize are almost
always found in the form of isolated kernels, often associated with
basketry fragments or ceramic vessels.

        Three types of maize were recovered from AZ BB:13:146: Onaveno,
a 10-12 rowed flint corn; Mais Blando, a 10-12 rowed flour corn; and
Harinoso de Ocho, a large-kerneled, 8-rowed flour corn. All three types

Table 4. Nonwood plant remains from AZ BB:13:146

Sample Number	Context	Sample Volume (unfloated-liters)	Sample Weight (floated-gms.)	Maize Kernels	% Onaveno	% Mais Blando	% Harinoso de Ocho	Beans	Pigweed Seeds	Grass Stems
Flotation Samples:										
1	Pit house fill	4	9.5	2	+	-	-	3 f	5	-
2	Feature 4	9	143.1	502 ml	-	60	40	-	3 ml	-
3	Feature 3	5	19.5	44 ml	18	45	36	1 ff	4	2
4	Pit house fill	5	22.4	30 ml	20	53	27	3 ff	33	-
5	Feature 5	2	1.5	2	+	-	-	-	5	-
Macrofossil Identifications:										
6	Feature 4		6	-	-	33	67	-	-	-
12	Pit house floor		30 ml	-	-	30	70	-	-	-

f indicates fragments of cotyledons

ff indicates numerous fragments

+ = present

Table 5. Wood charcoal from AZ BB:13:146

Sample Number	Context	Relative Amount of Wood Charcoal	Number of Fragments					
			Cottonwood	Mesquite	Blue Palo-Verde	Foothills Palo-Verde	Greythorn	Desert Willow
Flotation Samples:								
1	Pit house fill	E	-	-	-	-	-	-
2	Feature 4	A	2	3	4	1	2	-
3	Feature 3	A	-	-	-	1	-	-
4	Pit house fill	A	1	-	-	1	-	-
5	Feature 5	E	-	-	-	-	-	-
Macrofossil Identifications:								
10	Pit house fill		-	-	1	-	-	-
11	Floor contact		-	-	-	-	-	2
	Site Total		3	3	5	3	2	2
	% of Wood Charcoal		17	17	28	17	11	11

E = Trace

A = Abundant

of maize also were recovered from the St. Mary's Hospital Site (Table 6) and were still grown by the Papago in the early 1900s (Miksicek 1979). Only Mais Blando, called Papago White Flour or Papago "60 Day Corn," is still grown to any extent on the reservation today. In contrast to the collection of maize from the St. Mary's Site which was mostly Onaveno with some Mais Blando, AZ BB:13:146 was dominated by the more palatable, floury forms, Harinoso de Ocho and Mais Blando. The difference might be attributable to the numerous dry farming features associated with the St. Mary's Site (Masse 1979) which would have been suited to the more drought-resistant, Onaveno-type maize. Mais Blando and Harinoso de Ocho would grow better on irrigated floodplains, or in floodwater fields.

A curious sampling bias is evident in the AZ BB:13:146 maize collection. The hand-picked macrofossil samples SN 6 and SN 12 are dominated by the larger-kerneled form, Harinoso de Ocho, whereas the flotation samples have much higher proportions of Mais Blando. The larger kernels are more visible and easier to pick up. This bias should be considered in future archaeobotanical work.

Carbonized beans are very difficult to assign to any cultivated variety, as the most diagnostic features are seed-coat color and patterning which are lost upon carbonization (Kaplan 1956). Metric data is difficult to work with as different varieties of beans respond to charring in different ways; some shrink, some swell. Personal experimentation and information from Leonard W. Blake show that length tends to decrease, whereas width and thickness tend to increase. Much depends on the moisture content of the bean when it is charred. Because of these considerations, the varietal identifications in Table 4 and the following discussion should be considered tentative at best. The variability in size and shape in the intact cotyledons from AZ BB:13:146 suggest three distinct cultivars. The bean from SN 3 is flattened with truncate ends suggesting that it is probably a tepary bean, _Phaseolus acutifolius_ var. _latifolius_. It is quite similar to teparies recovered from the St. Mary's Site (Miksicek 1979). The two beans from SN 4, tentatively labeled C20, are larger, elliptical, and have entire margins. They are quite similar to beans from Kukendahl, near Nogales, Arizona, and from Montezuma's Castle described by Kaplan (1956). The other bean from SN 4 is larger and subreniform, possibly a C15 type as described by Kaplan (1956). Both C20 and C15 are common beans, _Phaseolus vulgaris_.

The recovery of maize, beans, and amaranth seeds from AZ BB:13:146, and the absence of any other seasonal indicators, suggests that these remains were deposited in the late summer or early fall, when all of these plant foods would be available. This does not preclude utilization of the site during other seasons.

Nutritional Complementation of Maize, Beans, and Amaranth

The co-occurrence of maize, beans, and amaranth in the flotation samples from AZ BB:13:146 led me to wonder about the protein content of these three plant foods. Protein complementation of grains and legumes is a common feature of native diets worldwide.

There are 8-10 essential amino acids which cannot be synthesized in the mammalian body and must be obtained in the diet. These are listed in Table 6. The amino acid complementation of the New World maize-and-beans combination is well known. Corn, like many grains, is deficient in lysine and tryptophan. Beans, on the other hand, have high proportions of these two amino acids, but are lacking in the sulfur-containing amino

Table 6. Archaeological maize from the Tucson Basin

Race	Analyzed Kernels	% of Total Sample	Row Number	Kernel Width (mm)	Kernel Thickness (mm)	Reconstructed Ear Diameter (mm)
AZ BB:13:146						
Onaveno	8	8	none measurable			
Mais Blando	44	47	10.3	7.5	5.1	31.1
S.D. ±			1.06	.50	.50	3.10
Harinoso de Ocho	42	45	8.1	8.7	5.5	26.6
S.D. ±			.48	.51	.46	1.96
St. Mary's Site (AZ AA:16:26)						
Onaveno			9.7	6.8	4.5	
Mais Blando			10.0	7.5	5.2	
Harinoso de Ocho			8.0	9.6	6.0	

S.D. = Standard deviation

Table 7. Beans from AZ BB:13:146 and comparative data

Specimens	Cotyledon Length (mm)	Cotyledon Width (mm)	Seed Thickness (mm)	Comments
BB:13:146 SN 3 T5(?)	8.4	5.2	4.8	charred
BB:13:146 SN 4 C20(?)	9.5	5.9	6.0	charred
	9.4	5.4	5.4	charred
BB:13:146 SN 4 C15(?)	10.9	6.9	5.4	charred
St. Mary's T5(?)	8.3	5.6	4.2	charred, A.D. 700-1100
Kaplan's T5 Type	8.9	6.0	4.3	modern
Montezuma's Castle C20	9.4	5.9	4.3	uncharred, A.D. 1300
Kukendahl C20, Nogales	8.9	6.2	4.3	charred, A.D. 1200-1450
Kaplan's C20 Type	9.3	5.9	4.3	modern
Kaplan's C15 Type	10.8	6.5	4.3	modern

acids, methionine and cystine, and somewhat low in the aromatic amino acids phenylalanine and tyrosine. Maize, in turn, compensates for this deficiency with high levels of these amino acids. Eaten together, maize and beans give complete protein with all essential amino acids. This grain-legume pattern is seen worldwide. Other examples are wheat and lentils in the Near East, millet and soybeans in northern China, rice and mung beans in Southeast Asia, and sorghum and cowpeas in East Africa. Primitive people may have had a concept equivalent to proteins, but they certainly didn't know about amino acids which were not discovered until 1820. Partially by serendipity, native populations discovered the food combinations that gave the most complete diet. Undoubtedly, another factor was natural selection. Populations with better diets were more healthy and more reproductively fit. These groups survived longer and produced more offspring.

The data in Tables 6 and 7 were assembled from Downton (1973), Senft (1980), and Duke (1981). Normally, proteins are compared to an "ideal protein," and hen's egg is usually used as a standard. The LAA is the "Limiting Amino Acid" score, calculated as the ratio of the proportion of the most deficient amino acid of a food to its proportion in the standard, multiplied by 100 to give a whole number. The EAA is the

138

Table 8. A comparison of the nutritional value of maize, beans, and amaranth

	Percent Protein	IAA	EAA	Cal./100 gms	Limiting Amino Acids	Other Key Nutrients
Phaseolus vulgaris (seeds)	20.3	64	90	333	Methionine, Cystine	Potassium, Iron, Phosphorus
Zea mays (seeds)	9-13	35	86	361	Lysine, Tryptophan	Thiamine, Niacin
Amaranthus spp. (seeds)	13.5-17.5	67	85	426	Leucine, Isoleucine, Valine, Threonine	Oil, Phosphorous, Calcium
Amaranthus (greens)	3.5	37	91	36	Methionine, Cystine	Iron, Calcium, Vitamins A and C

Table 9. Essential amino acid composition of maize, beans, and amaranth (% of protein)

	Tryptophan	Methionine/ Cystine	Isoleucine	Threonine	Valine	Lysine	Phenylalanine/ Tyrosine	Leucine
Beans	1.2	1.0	6.3	4.3	6.2	8.1	5.5	8.0
Maize	0.6	3.2	4.6	4.0	5.1	1.9	10.6	13.0
Amaranth (seeds)	1.2-1.5	4.0-4.8	2.8-3.2	2.7-3.0	3.3-3.8	4.8-5.0	6.0-6.6	4.4-5.0
Amaranth (greens)	1.2	1.3	5.3	4.5	7.0	5.9	5.5	9.2
FAO/WHO Standard	1.0	3.5	4.0	4.0	5.0	5.5	6.0	7.0

Note: Underlined values are of the most limiting amino acid

"Essential Amino Acid" score, which is the average of all the proportions of each amino acid to its proportion in the standard, multiplied by 100. In calculating the EAA when the proportion of a given amino acid in a food exceeds that in the standard, the ratio is set at 1.0. Both "Percent Protein" and "Calories/gm" are based on fresh weight.

From Tables 8 and 9, it can be seen that amaranth seeds are deficient in leucine, isoleucine, threonine, and valine, but they have more of the sulfur-containing amino acids than either beans or maize. Sulfur-containing amino acids are very important as hydrogen bonds between adjacent sulfur molecules. These molecules create the three-dimensional structure of proteins which is a key factor in enzyme activity. Amaranth seeds compensate for low levels of lysine and tryptophan in maize or methionine/cystine and phenylalanine/tyrosine in beans. A diet consisting of amaranth seeds and maize alone would be complete in all essential amino acids. Beans, maize, and amaranth seeds together provide very comlete, high-quality protein.

Although the overall protein content of amaranth greens is low, they contain all essential amino acids except, rather curiously, methionine and cystine which are high in the seeds. In early summer when amaranth greens would be available and when the aboriginal diet was dominated by carbohydrates in the form of mesquite pods and saguaro fruits, amaranth greens would provide some needed protein and other important nutrients such as iron, calcium, and vitamins A and C. Later in the season, amaranth seeds would supplement the maize-beans diet with oil, phosphorus, and calcium.

When wild foods such as amaranth are considered along with the maize-beans-squash diet of the Hohokam, it becomes apparent that the pre-historic inhabitants of southern Arizona had a nutritionally complete diet available to them. Although there were certainly calorically lean times, such as early spring when stored food reserves would be low and wild foods limited, it is possible to look at aboriginal diets in the Southwest in terms of "feast" rather than "famine."

APPENDIX B

POLLEN EVIDENCE FROM AZ BB:13:146

Suzanne K. Fish
Arizona State Museum
The University of Arizona

A pit house and two associated pit features furnished samples for pollen analysis at AZ BB:13:146. Pollen was extracted from the soil matrix using a heavy liquid flotation method. A swirl technique (Mehringer 1967:136-137) preceded further separation of the pollen bearing fraction with zinc bromide. Identifications were made at a magnification of 500x to a total of 200 grains for each sample.

The three samples are dominated by nonarboreal pollen types, with Cheno-Ams (pollen of the Chenopod family plus the genus Amaranthus) the most frequent. While some of the chenopods and amaranths producing this pollen may have been responding to the disturbed habitat around human habitations, the prominence of this pollen type is also predictable in desert floodplain settings (Hevly, Mehringer and Yocum 1965; Martin 1963; Schoenwetter and Doerschlag 1971). Vegetation directly on the site was most probably open, with both creosote-bush (Larrea) and mesquite (Prosopis) communities nearby. Creosote-bush is a typical member of basin floor associations. The mesquite bosque suggested by the flotation results and by the abundance of chenopods and amaranths are more closely associated with the environs of drainages.

A pollen type appearing in both Feature 3 and Feature 4 reveals the presence of permanently wet conditions, perhaps in Tanque Verde Wash. Cattail (Typha) pollen occurred in small amounts in the two samples. Cattails provide both food and craft materials; gathered plants may have introduced the pollen. The additional evidence of cottonwood charcoal in the flotation remains also argues for a permanently damp riparian community nearby, however. Such a situation could have been localized within the wash by damming or ponding. Natural locales of more permanent water availability may have been enhanced by the intervention of humans or beavers. Other instances of cattail pollen have been reported from sites in the Tucson area, such as that at Whiptail Ruin (Lytle-Webb 1978).

Economic types in the pollen at AZ BB:13:146 include corn (Zea) and cucurbits (Cucurbita). The Feature 1 cucurbit pollen, from a pit house floor, could have been produced by either cultivated squash or gourds or the small gathered gourds Cucurbita foetidissima and Cucurbita digitata.

Table 10. Percentages of pollen types in samples from AZ BB:13:146

Provenience	Sample Number	Sample Size	Ambrosia-type	Other Low Spine Compositae	High Spine Compositae	Cheno-Am	Gramineae	Plantago	Euphorbia-type	Sphaeralcea	Boerhaavia-type	Eriogonum	Caryophyllaceae	Larrea	Prosopis	Other Leguminosae	Pinus	Quercus	Ephedra	Typha	Unknown Types	Cucurbita	Zea
F.3 pit fill Strat. 1 .48-.58 MBD	8	200	2	15.5	12	54	2.5	7.5	2	2	-	-	-	.5	-	-	1	-	-	1	-	-	1
F.4 pit fill Strat. 1 .50-.82 MBD	9	200	1.5	16	14.5	49.5	3.5	-	3.5	-	-	.5	-	-	1	.5	5	-	.5	.5	3.5	-	-
F.1 pit house floor N4E6-43 MBD	7	200	3.5	18	18.5	34.5*	2	-	2.5	-	1	1.5	7.5	-	-	8	.5	.5	-	-	2	1	2

*aggregates present

Corn pollen was recovered from the pit house floor and from Feature 3.
The low frequencies strengthen a conclusion of storage in the form of
kernels, derived from the absence of cobs in the floated materials. It
seems likely that the corn was husked and cut from the cobs elsewhere, and
transported to the site as kernels with little pollen adhering. Perhaps
the first steps in processing were performed at a field site.

Cheno-Am pollen also appears to have an economic component.
Although the pit house yielded the lowest percentage of Cheno-Am pollen,
aggregates were present. These clumps of pollen are probably the result
of plant parts brought into the pit house, since aggregated grains would
not be easily transported by air. Pigweed seeds identified from several
site proveniences very likely result from the same resource use.

Two additional pollen types indicate gathered plants. Each
palynologically rare type pertains to plants which might have been present
in the natural vegetation, but anomalous distributions suggest human introduction. <u>Plantago</u> pollen occurs only in Feature 3. Seeds of species,
called Indian Wheat, were gathered and eaten ethnographically. Pollen of
the pink family, Caryophyllaceae, was found only on the pit house floor.
A more specific identification was not possible. These plants were
probably used as medicinals.

REFERENCES

Castetter, Edward F., and William H. Bell
  1942   Pima and Papago Indian Agriculture. Albuquerque: University
           of New Mexico Press.

Cattanach, George S., Jr.
  1966   A San Pedro stage site near Fairbank, Arizona. The Kiva
           32(1):1-24.

Downton, W. J. S.
  1973   Amaranthus edulis: A high lysine grain amaranth. World Crops
           25:20.

Duke, James A.
  1981   Handbook of Legumes of World Economic Importance. New York:
           Plenum Press.

Gibb, James, and Barbara Hall
  1981   Archaeological Testing at Pulte Home Speedway East 40 Develop-
           ment Area. Letter Report to Pulte Home Corporation. Cultural
           Resource Management Division, Arizona State Museum, University
           of Arizona, Tucson.

Huckell, Bruce B.
  1980   The ANAMAX-Rosemont testing project. MS, Cultural Resource
           Management Division, Arizona State Museum, University of
           Arizona, Tucson.

Kaplan, Lawrence
  1956   The cultivated beans of the prehistoric Southwest. Annals of
           the Missouri Botanical Garden 43:87-188.

Kelly, Isabel T., James E. Officer, and Emil W. Haury
  1978   The Hodges Ruin: A Hohokam community in the Tucson Basin.
           Anthropological Papers of the University of Arizona 30.
           Tucson: University of Arizona Press.

Lytle-Webb, Jamie
  1978   Pollen analysis in southwestern archaeology. In Discovering
           Past Behavior: Experiments in the Archaeology of the American
           Southwest, edited by P. Brebinger. New York: Gordon and
           Breach.

Greenleaf, J. Cameron
  1975   Excavations at Punta de Agua, in the Santa Cruz River basin,
            southeastern Arizona. Anthropological Papers of the University
            of Arizona 26. Tucson: University of Arizona Press.

Haury, Emil W.
  1975   The Stratigraphy and Archaeology of Ventana Cave (Second
            Edition). Tucson: University of Arizona Press.

  1976   The Hohokam, Desert Farmers and Craftsmen: Excavation at
            Snaketown, 1964-1965. Tucson: University of Arizona Press.

Hevly, Richard H., P. J. Mehringer, and H. G. Yocum
  1965   Modern pollen rain in the Sonoran Desert. Journal of the
            Arizona Academy of Science 3:123-135.

Martin, Paul S.
  1963   The Last 10,000 Years. Tucson: University of Arizona Press.

Masse, W. Bruce
  1979   An intensive survey of prehistoric dry farming systems near
            Tumamoc Hill in Tucson, Arizona. The Kiva 45(1-2):141-186.

Mehringer, P. J.
  1967   Pollen analysis of the Tule Springs area, Nevada. In "Pleisto-
            cene Studies in Southern Nevada," edited by H. Wormington and
            D. Ellis. Nevada State Museum Anthropological Papers 13(3):
            120-200.

Miksicek, Charles H.
  1979   From parking lots to museum basements: The archaeobotany of
            the St. Mary's Site. The Kiva 45(1-2):131-140.

Miksicek, Charles H. and Suzanne K. Fish
  1981   Understanding aboriginal subsistence activities in southern
            Arizona. Paper delivered at the 4th Ethnobiology Conference,
            Columbia, Missouri.

Pearsall, Deborah M.
  1980   Analysis of an archaeological maize kernel cache from Manabi
            Province, Ecuador. Economic Botany 34:344-351.

Schoenwetter, James and L. Doerschlag
  1971   Surficial pollen records from central Arizona 1: Sonoran
            desert scrub. Journal of the Arizona Academy of Science
            6:216-221.

Senft, Joseph P.
  1980   Protein quality of amaranth grain. Proceedings of the Second
            Amaranth Conference, pp. 43-47. Emmaus, PA: Rodale Press.